STILL DREAMING

Another Year in the Life of a Premier League Club

Alex Fynn and Martin Cloake

HAWKSMOOR
PUBLISHING

First published 2023 by Hawksmoor Publishing

Woodside, Oakamoor, ST10 3AE, UK

www.hawksmoorpublishing.com

ISBN: 978-1-914066-18-4

To the memory of Tony Fuller (aka H. Davidson), a gentleman and fine writer; Morris Keston, whose kindness and generosity was valued by countless players, especially Spurs'; David Stern, a true fan and friend; and Kevin Fitzgerald, a good man who made a difference.

THE AUTHORS

As a Director of Saatchi & Saatchi, Alex Fynn advised the FA, the Football League and several Premier League clubs, including Tottenham Hotspur, on media and marketing. He was awarded an honorary Doctorate by Solent University in 2022. Together with H. Davidson, he wrote *Dream On,* described by *FourFourTwo* as "a football classic".

Martin Cloake is a journalist, editor and Tottenham Hotspur season ticket holder. He has worked on a number of award-winning books about the club, is co-author of *A People's History of THFC,* the first book to tell the story of a club through the history of its supporters, and writes regularly about the culture and business of football. He currently works as a business journalist.

Also by Alex Fynn and Martin Cloake: *One Step From Glory* – The story of Tottenham Hotspur's Champions League campaign 2018/19.

ACKNOWLEDGEMENTS

This book could not have happened without the invaluable help of many people. First and foremost, James Lumsden-Cook for his support, enthusiasm and skilful editing; and Katrina Law and Jonny Blain, for their eagle eyes in spotting countless errors and their pertinent suggestions. Gratitude is owed to Irving Scholar, Douglas Alexiou, Edward Freedman, Doug Bagley and Danny Kelly for their insights, and to Douglas Alexiou for reading the manuscript.

As a source of inspiration and information *The Athletic* has brought a new depth and breadth to reporting and analysing football; *The Deloitte Annual Report of Football Finance* remains the most important review of the industry; Swiss Ramble's expert financial analysis and several podcasts, especially *The View from the Lane, The Spurs Show,* and *The Price of Football* were always instructive and entertaining. Alan Fisher's *Tottenham On My Mind* blog, *The Fighting Cock, Echoes of Glory,* Adam Powley, Annelise Jespersen, Ali Pugh, Bruce Lee and all the matchday crew have all been a rich source of fan sentiment and good company in testing times.

Special mention must go to Rhoda Fynn, who again spent hours compensating for her husband's IT inadequacies, and to Cath, Danny and Tom for their understanding.

To all, we owe thanks.

CONTENTS

INTRODUCTION

'We (Spurs) need to be dreamers because if you are dreamers that can bring you something incredible in your life.' Antonio Conte, August 2022

In 1996, Alex Fynn and the still much-missed Tony Fuller (aka H Davidson) wrote a book called *Dream On*. It chronicled a year in the life of a Premier League club in what was then the fifth season of the Premier League.

Those were different days, but the direction of travel was established. Spurs had been one of the instigators of the new era, but – as it turns out – they failed to benefit from what they had helped to create for many years. *Dream On* reads now as a chronicle of a club losing touch with the modern world.

The introduction to *Dream On* said, 'In telling the story of one club, we are really telling the story of English Premier League football today.' The current authors hope that our story will similarly interest the general reader, but once again, Spurs has been chosen because of our affinity with the club. We've also stayed true to the task the authors set in *Dream On*, which is to tell the story in real-time, an approach set out in that book as follows,

1

'Written as the season unfolded, we were sometimes overtaken by events that left us looking either mistaken or, occasionally, prescient. However, a decision was taken at the outset not to be masters of hindsight. We hope that the reader will acknowledge our policy not to rewrite each chapter, but instead view each as a snapshot of the situation at that moment in time.

'This is not a match-by-match account of the season, rather a journey through the issues that shape today's game, using the chronology of a season to lead from one event to the next. We have tried to offer solutions rather than snipe, although we fear most criticism may be unwelcomed by the recipients, but we hope our words can be accepted in the constructive vein in which they are offered.'

Twenty-six years after *Dream On* was published, Tottenham Hotspur is still dreaming.

1. CLOSE ... AND A
SMALL CIGAR

Gambolling in the Norfolk sunshine was not how it was expected to end. As Antonio Conte and his players basked in the warmth of the late spring weather and the appreciation of the estimated 7,000 Spurs fans who had made the journey to Carrow Road for the final game of the 2021/22 season, it was hard to grasp just how unlikely this outcome had once seemed.

Perhaps the greatest irony was that a club that had, just 13 months before, tried to set up a breakaway, closed European Super League (ESL)[1] was now celebrating qualification to a competition it had tried to sabotage from a league it had twice wanted to

---

[1] It took just three days for an unholy alliance of European billionaires, Russian oligarchs, Middle East nation-states, and US hedge funds to see their plans for a breakaway league of 20 of the game's biggest clubs, with the 16 founder members guaranteed a perpetual place, come crashing down after fierce resistance from governments, UEFA, and most of all, fans.

wreck, firstly with Project Big Picture[2] and then with the ESL. A year is a lifetime in football.

Tottenham Hotspur had wasted the first three months of the season after a bungled search for a new manager had led to the appointment of a man widely perceived to be, at best, the board's fourth or fifth choice. Nuno Espirito Santo lasted just three months until his departure; an opening weekend win over Manchester City already a distant memory for a team that didn't run, didn't create, and didn't believe in itself. A 3-0 home defeat by Manchester United on the 30th of October proved to be the final straw and ensured the two Manchester sides bookended the curtailed Nuno era.

In came Antonio Conte, the man said to have been Spurs' first choice. Had the club not tried hard

---

[2] Driven by Manchester United and Liverpool, with support from Manchester City, Chelsea, Tottenham and Arsenal, Project Big Picture was a cynical manoeuvre to exploit the financial distress caused by Covid-19. It comprised an offer of £250 million to the Football League (EFL) from the Premier League in return for a reduction of the top league to 18 clubs, the abolition of the League Cup and Community Shield, and the acceptance of special voting rights for the Big Six. Why the greedy six thought their fellow members would vote away their power is beyond belief.

enough to get him, or had he simply not wanted to come? Whatever had or hadn't happened in the summer, the question – as autumn slipped away into winter – was what, if anything, had changed to make someone with one of the most successful track records in world club football – he had just resigned from Internazionale after leading them to their first Serie A title in a decade – come to a club that, frankly, hadn't matched his achievements?

While the appointment of a manager (or in his employer's nomenclature 'head coach') of Conte's stature was undeniably a boost, there was also a sense that all that was needed was to sit back and wait for the inevitable implosion. Conte was high-maintenance, not averse to speaking out in public, demanding big-money backing, and not settling for mediocrity. All qualities guaranteed to sit uneasily with Spurs chairman Daniel Levy, whose own obdurate reputation reinforced the feeling that those settling back and waiting for the fireworks would not be disappointed.

Conte's tenure began unspectacularly, with a chaotic 3-2 victory over Vitesse Arnhem in the Europa Conference League, followed by an uninspiring goalless draw against Everton. Points were at least racked up in the league, but an ignominious loss against Slovenian minnows NS Mura left qualification from the group stage of Europe's third-tier contest hanging by a thread. In the event, Spurs were kicked out for being unable to field a team for the final tie against Rennes due to a Covid-19 outbreak – the club's protestations about the injustice of it all never quite convincing anyone that they weren't heartily glad to be out of the tournament.

As a fresh wave of Covid-19 prompted postponements, the season stuttered, and there were fears that recovery from the last stoppage would be swept away. But action resumed late in December with a game of extraordinary quality and intensity against a rampant Liverpool at the Tottenham Hotspur Stadium that finished all square, 2-2, but from which Spurs could, maybe should, have emerged victorious. It was the first real sign of the Conte effect.

However, January proved a testing month. A nervy three points away at Watford and a remarkable injury-time 3-2 win at Leicester were counterbalanced by a demoralising treble of defeats in the league and League Cup against Conte's old side, and Spurs' *bête noire* in blue, Chelsea.

January is also the month of the mid-season transfer window; a new manager's first chance to stamp his mark. After the tiresome swirl of rumour and reaction that now passes for sports journalism in some parts of the English media had passed, Spurs were left with two in and four out. Dejan Kulusevski and Rodrigo Bentancur arrived, while Tanguy

Ndombele, Bryan Gil, Giovanni Lo Celso, and Dele Alli all left.

Many fans were left underwhelmed. An already stretched squad had been reduced in number. The new signings suggested the much-vaunted contacts of Managing Director of Football, 'Don' Fabio Paratici, extended only as far as his former club Juventus, and the departure on loan of the diminutive Gil – signed only that summer by Paratici – cast further doubts on a recruitment strategy that had been falling short for some time. Ndombele and Lo Celso had been strongly backed by former manager Mauricio Pochettino, while Alli had been a fans' favourite and a stalwart of a great side that was halted one step from glory. So much significance could be read into the arrivals and departures, but the bare facts were that four players who were clearly not part of Conte's plans had been moved out, albeit on loan, while two he saw as capable of coming straight into the first team had been brought in.

When the players celebrated on that final May day, against Norwich, no Spurs fan watching doubted the quality of the two incomers. 'Kulu', serenaded to the tune of kitsch ABBA classic *Gimme, Gimme, Gimme*, had scored twice; Bentancur had proved instrumental in running the five-goal show, and Son Heung-Min – a player previously written off by many after an indifferent first season at the club – had scored twice to tie with Liverpool's Mohammed Salah with 23 goals (none from the penalty spot) as the Premier League's Golden Boot winner.

But football turns on fine margins, and the combination of money, money, money and intensity of coverage in the modern game encourages every reaction to be amplified. It is, as The Persuaders once told us, a thin line between love and hate. If Spurs, as some had feared, had fallen short on that final day, missing out on the Champions League and finishing behind Arsenal of all clubs, the levels of toxicity might have more than matched the levels of joy. January's transfer window would have been labelled a disaster. Calls for the club's owners to go would have intensified, as would disputes between supporters. The narrative about choking, snatching defeat from the jaws of victory, would have been seen once more as a salient characteristic of the club's DNA.

Nevertheless, sober reflection, of which one suspects there was not much that night, makes it hard to avoid the conclusion that Tottenham Hotspur's fourth-place finish was a remarkable achievement. The first three months of the season had been thrown away and the club's decline from the good-time heights of the Pochettino years looked set to accelerate. There had appeared to be no cohesion, direction, or sense of identity. And yet, as the curtain fell on the season's drama, all of that was back. Since his arrival, Conte had won more league points (56) than anyone except Jürgen Klopp (70) or

Pep Guardiola (73). Following defeat to Middlesbrough in the fifth round of the FA Cup in March, Spurs had won nine and drawn two.

The run included a hugely gratifying 3-0 drubbing of a hapless Arsenal, who were in the driving seat for fourth place after Spurs had unexpectedly dropped five points over two games against Brighton and Brentford. The satisfaction of the derby win was enhanced by the circumstances in which it took place. Arsenal had managed to get the scheduled fixture in January postponed, claiming not to have had 'the necessary players' available due to Covid-19. The game was eventually rearranged for the penultimate week of the season on the 12th of May at the behest of Sky (whose determination to create rather than just transmit events provided further illustration that the television tail wags the football dog). Ironically, Arsenal's selection options were curtailed by injury and suspension, while Spurs could call on two of the signings of the season in Kulusevski and Bentancur, who would not have been available had the match gone ahead in its original slot.

On an evening when the fans finally put an end to complaints that Tottenham's magnificent new stadium was incapable of generating a hostile atmosphere, Arsenal were exposed as the kind of brittle outfit Spurs had so often proved to be when under pressure.

It was a victory that would live long in the memory, and followed another titanic tussle at Anfield the previous week (a game which many pundits thought would leave Spurs trailing their London rivals by five points when they met). But the 1-1 draw left Spurs as the only team not to have lost to either of the top two sides in the final table. A team that during one bleak period of the season couldn't muster a shot on target in match after match had ultimately scored 70 goals; a team that had covered less ground than any other had run further than most; a team that had looked bereft had discovered new impetus.

*

Monday dawned bright after the final Super Sunday of the Premier League season, but for Spurs fans, the unexpected delight escalated with an announcement as extraordinary as the team's achievement on the pitch. ENIC, the club's owners, were to put £150 million into the club, as working capital. Plainly, at least in part, to bolster Conte's transfer chest. The move was as radical as it was unexpected.

In the 21 years in which it had controlled the club, ENIC had very firmly stuck to the principle of self-sufficiency, that the club would be run as a business. The strategy had become increasingly onerous to maintain as competitors were bankrolled by oligarchs and nation-states for whom red figures on the balance sheet were irrelevant, or for savvy investors such as the Fenway Sports Group, owners of two – Liverpool and the Boston Red Sox – of the most successful clubs in sport.

Between 2011-16, Spurs' net transfer spending was the miserly sum of £8 million. During this period, and until the pandemic struck, substantial profits were recorded. In 2018 and 2019, indeed, there were record profits of over £200 million. The money enabled the club to reduce both the amount and cost of borrowing to offset the over £1 billion spent on the new training facilities in Enfield and the Tottenham Hotspur Stadium. Long-term loans at affordable rates were negotiated so that, after 2016, the club was able to throw caution to the wind and become net spenders to the tune of over £200 million. But the pandemic hit, and Spurs lost £67.7 million. Manchester City lost more than £125 million and Liverpool more than £52 million, but this was a severe blow for Spurs.

Despite the deficit, nobody could doubt Spurs was a well-run business, but the criticism often levelled at the club's owners was that the business considerations were promoted to such an extent that the chance to push on in sporting terms was missed. Under Harry Redknapp and again under Pochettino, arguably the club's best manager in a generation, the chance to prioritise prizes had been spurned, and the fear was that the same might happen again.

'Back Conte' was the call from the fans, and Conte was certainly not averse to encouraging speculation that he would walk if he felt he was not being wholeheartedly endorsed. Even in his short time in charge, he'd blown up on camera several times, questioning the wisdom of staying at the club and the ability of the players and owners to deliver the goods. Those outbursts were lapped up not only by the media but by the proliferating fan channels on social media that thrive on controversy and division. Frequent, boorish conduct is not confined to football – the business models of the social media giants are predicated on the basis that extreme opinion and controversy boost user figures, and the same principles have been deployed to public and political discourse with depressingly predictable results, leaving a constant, lamentable backdrop against which any attempt at conversation is played out.

Conte's comments cannot have gone down well in a boardroom averse to airing any linen at all in public – unless it suited its purpose. But even here, there must have been the realisation that if Conte went, that would mean two of the most successful managers of the modern era – remember José Mourinho? – had failed. Therefore, the inescapable conclusion regarding the board would be that, to quote the classic old brush-off, 'It's not me, it's you'.

But while the need to back Conte must have been a vital consideration, it is unlikely to have been the only factor in ENIC's decision to break with the habit of a lifetime at Spurs and put its own money into the club. Take a step back, and there were solid business reasons why choosing that moment to invest made sense, and only some of them rooted in a recognition that opportunities may have been spurned before.

By finishing fourth, Spurs were guaranteed a minimum of £35 million just by qualifying for the Champions League group stage. That's before matchday revenues in 21/22 of £106 million. In 2019, the prize money earned from the club's run to the Champions League final was £94 million. Factor in broadcast and commercial revenue and, after a successful run in Europe, one could be looking at a total turnover approaching £500 million. If that is repeated year on year, Spurs will begin to secure an advantage over any opponent not owned by a nation-state or oligarch (the free-spending Real Madrid, Barcelona and Bayern Munich excepted).

After the termination of Roman Abramovich's 19-year reign in May 2022, Chelsea was no longer owned by an oligarch. And for all the fine talk of the club's new owners, the Todd Boehly consortium, the reality was that, for the first time in many years, Chelsea would be run as a business – a major shareholder is an American private equity company whose *raison d'etre* is profit. Though with a commitment to spend £1.75 billion, in addition to the purchase price of £2.5 billion, manager Thomas Tuchel would not lack funds.

Another rival, Arsenal, faced a sixth consecutive season outside the Champions League. That exacts a price not just in cumulative financial terms, but in reputational terms too. By securing fourth place ahead of the old enemy on that final day, Spurs not only gained bragging rights, for what they are worth, but more significantly potentially shifted the balance of power in North London for some time to come.

And what of Manchester United? The final day saw the fifth-largest club in the world only scrape into the Europa League. The team was in disarray and a new manager, Erik ten Hag, and a new CEO, Richard Arnold, had huge rebuilding tasks facing them. The owners, the Glazer family, had made no secret of their use of the club as a cash cow, so what would happen if the udders dried up? Writing off a club the size and stature of Manchester United would be foolish, but in the immediate future its ability to compete at the top on the pitch would at best be a work in progress.

That left Chelsea and, of course, Manchester City, Liverpool, and potentially Newcastle United as contenders for a top-four place. The latter was in the early days of untold wealth courtesy of its majority shareholder, the Public Investment Fund of Saudi Arabia, which bought the club in October 2021. But it could take some time to create the kind of structure that has to combine with financial power to create a successful team and convince some of the world's top talent that Tyneside is the place to be.

Although Chelsea defeated Spurs on four occasions in 2021/2022, the true test for Spurs looked as if it would come from Manchester City, who can outspend everyone as befits their status at the head of the Deloitte Money League, and Liverpool, who are not only a huge brand but a footballing machine capable of firing the imagination; they were, after all, one point and one goal away from finishing the season with a unique quadruple (Premier League, Champions League, FA Cup and League Cup). However, in their one-to-one encounters, Spurs had matched or bettered them both.

If not now, then *when* would there be a more opportune time to see if Spurs really had what it takes to challenge for the title and – at the very least – widen the gap between them and the chasing pack for a Champions League place?

The announcement on Monday the 23rd of May was that ENIC was paying £150 million to increase its stake in the club from 85.6% to 87.5%. With 213 million existing shares, 32 million new shares needed to be issued, making the value of the club around £1.1 billion. And yet a price of £2.5 billion had just been agreed for the purchase of Chelsea. A club whose antiquated home with a capacity of 41,000 would bring in less than half the matchday revenue of its North London rival; a club that didn't possess a state-of-the-art training facility and could no longer expect to be bankrolled by an infinitely open chequebook.

If the owners asked themselves what Chelsea had that Spurs didn't, there was an obvious answer: trophies. And the result of winning the Champions League and the World Club Championship enabled Chelsea to weather the Covid-19 storm, proving the point many fans had been making for many years: that sporting success underpinned everything. No doubt Levy would argue that sporting success could only be achieved on a successful business basis, but the entry of nation-states, oligarchs, and American sports entrepreneurs has changed the equation. It may be more accurate to argue that to have a successful business, you first have to have a successful team.

In a nutshell, finishing fourth in the circumstances that existed in May 2022 provided a clear sporting and business opportunity. The announcement of the cash injection indicated that the club was prepared to consider that chance. And that was a significant development.

As always, it was wise to read between the lines and exercise some caution. The cash injection 'may be drawn in tranches until the end of the year'. The new shares were 'convertible A shares' that could be converted into ordinary shares dependent on a number of other factors. 'If drawn in full', those shares 'could' see ENIC increase its ownership of the club. Those provisos could simply have been a means of balancing the interests of the (very limited number) of small shareholders and those of ENIC. Would this turn out to be another case of things not being quite what they seemed?

How this panned out would prove to be another fascinating chapter in the history of a club that, despite being in its most fallow period of trophy-winning since the 1930s, remained one of the most famous names in football. If trophies are so vital, should Spurs view the domestic cups as disdainfully as they have in recent seasons, or try to win one of any sort? Or should they go for the real prizes of the modern game, namely the Premier League title and the Champions League trophy, that still look out of reach?

Dreaming of success is something embedded in the club's character, back through Mauricio Pochettino, Keith Burkinshaw, Bill Nicholson, Danny Blanchflower, Arthur Rowe, Peter McWilliam, John Cameron; back to Bobby Buckle and the boys from Tottenham Grammar School who met under a streetlight on the High Road opposite where the stadium still stands and named a football club after a Shakespearean hero.

For the vital derby against Arsenal, as the teams took to the pitch, a huge *tifo* display across the 17,500-seater South Stand urged the players to 'Dare, Dream, Do'.

And they did.

Would the season 2022/23 see the dream finally realised?

2. LONG HOT SUMMER

Wildfires were breaking out, train tracks buckled, and the roads had begun to melt. Any doubts that human behaviour was contributing to significant changes in life were dispelled in a July that – on one broiling day – saw temperatures reach unprecedented levels of more than 40C in parts of the UK. Certainly not as unusual, but potentially as far-reaching, was the activity at Tottenham Hotspur as six new players arrived by the end of the month.

Since taking control of the club 21 years ago, the usual ENIC transfer market tactic had been to wait until as late as possible in the window to make a move to drive down the price of the targeted prospect. Chairman Daniel Levy was characterised – one suspects not without a little plausibly deniable encouragement from within the club – as a steel-nerved poker player ready to take every deal to the line to get the best price. The downside to the plan was that leaving it late often meant points dropped in the opening encounters that would ultimately prove costly in all senses at the end of the season; it would invariably be a few weeks into the campaign before the team gelled.

The arrival of a new breed of mega-rich owner fundamentally changed the landscape, though. Brinkmanship, once seen as a smart negotiating tool, now looked like timidity, indecision, or worse, an inability to compete. The infamous instance of two transfer windows in 2018 and 2019 with no deals made after Mauricio Pochettino had explicitly called for 'new furniture' was now what characterised the *modus operandi* of ENIC and Daniel Levy.

But in 2022, Antonio Conte's demeanour was also changing the climate. He'd made it clear that not only did he want signings made, but made early. And that he wanted reinforcements who could step straight into a first-team squad. What was conspicuous about the way he operated was that he'd made no bones about what he considered was right and what wasn't – effectively daring his employer to challenge his thinking. To paraphrase one of Elvis's biggest hits, based on an old Neapolitan melody, *O Sole Mio*, 'It's now or never, Conte won't wait'.

Tottenham Hotspur started to do business pretty swiftly. First to arrive was goalkeeper Fraser Forster from Southampton. It was a free transfer, and Forster would obviously be a backup for Hugo Lloris. An unexciting but sensible start, in contrast to another free transfer: Ivan Perišić from Internazionale.

One of the most exciting left-sided midfielders in Europe, Perišić was hugely experienced. He had represented Croatia on 113 occasions, including at the 2018 World Cup Final, and during his international career had scored 32 goals for his country. He was someone with whom Conte had worked before. At Internazionale in 2020/21, Perišić's willingness to adapt to life as a wing-back in Conte's system had been a key factor in the club securing the *Scudetto* (the title). Left wing-back was a position Spurs needed more depth in.

Two early signings then and, even more remarkably, both men were approaching their mid-thirties. No sell-on value to be found here – these were players brought in to do a job immediately. There was more to come.

Spurs splashed some of ENIC's much-vaunted cash injection on converting the loan of Cristian Romero from Atalanta into a permanent signing for €50m and on buying Yves Bissouma, who had been an impressive part of a Brighton & Hove Albion set-up that had been earning plaudits under manager Graham Potter. The £25 million fee looked to be a good deal for a midfielder viewed as possibly the best in his position outside the top six clubs. Spurs had brought in a versatile and tactically astute operator who would offer the kind of creative option needed to break down uncompromising opposition – something the team had often struggled to do. And he was only 25 years old.

Next to arrive was the Brazilian international forward Richarlison, secured after some more traditional Levy-style hard bargaining. Everton were deeply in debt. They had posted losses of over £100 million for three successive seasons from 2018 and so were desperately in need of funds to bring themselves in line with the Premier League's Profit and Sustainability rules and to provide their manager, Frank Lampard, with some purchasing power.

Reports suggested that Spurs had an initial £40 million bid turned down, but had come back with an offer of £50 million together with a further £10 million in add-ons. Everton simply couldn't refuse, even when the target was someone who had been indispensable for them in terms of goals scored, points won, shots made, and assists.

The transfer was significant not only because it was a big-money deal for a highly-rated, versatile Premier League stalwart, made well before the season started, but because it was hard to see Richarlison displacing any of a front three of Harry Kane, Son Heung-Min and Dejan Kulusevski in the starting eleven. Richarlison came to the club knowing he might not be first choice, but confident enough that he would get games. That said much about the new recruitment strategy. This was the kind of transfer that Spurs weren't prone to make; the kind that the biggest clubs habitually made.

As the month drew to a close, protracted negotiations for the much-fancied young right wing-back Djed Spence were concluded successfully. Spence had impressed in the Championship for his club Middlesbrough and also when on loan at Premier League-bound Nottingham Forest. A market rate fee of £13 million for a 21-year-old looked like value for money.

The final newcomer was 27-year-old Barcelona centre-back Clément Lenglet on loan. Conte had specifically asked for the France international to join his squad – another move to improve the strength in depth – despite the fact that the deal did not give Spurs an option to buy at the end of the year's loan.

So, in the week before the Premier League season kicked off, it was possible for the first time in many years for Spurs fans to see starting line-ups that would be a step up from the previous campaign, and to see top-class options from the bench – with five substitutions now permitted (bringing the Premier League belatedly in line with the rest of Europe) – who could influence outcomes rather than simply fill gaps.

Ironically, it was the wing-back positions, key to Conte's approach, that still seemed unresolved. On the left, the options were Perišić, who had made 49 appearances for Internazionale in the previous season but would surely not be expected to repeat that number for his new club; Ryan Sessegnon, who so far had not quite lived up to expectation; Sergio Reguilón, who Conte didn't seem to rate; and possibly Ben Davies, who didn't have the pace to be a top-drawer wing-back. On the right, the choices were Matt Doherty, who had shown signs of being the wing-back he'd been at his previous club,

Wolves, but had yet to hold down a starting spot; Emerson Royal, who had so far been unconvincing; the inexperienced Djed Spence; and Lucas Moura, who was only an outside bet to be a successful conversion from his striking role.

With the financial impact of Covid-19 felt by all clubs in 2019/20, the Premier League had bounced back to unprecedented heights the following season, attaining its highest ever revenue of £4.86 billion. Further, overseas broadcast rights, spearheaded by a £1 billion plus deal from the US, were set to exceed domestic deals for the first time. Together, total broadcast income for the Premier League, the richest sports league in the world, for the following three years was expected to top £10 billion, up from £8.5 billion (2019-2022).

The pandemic had widened the financial gap between the Premier League and the other major European leagues. Hitherto there were always a few clubs, such as Real Madrid, Barcelona, PSG, Bayern Munich, and Juventus, who were able to compete with their English peers in terms of transfers and wages. But the Premier League's €3.5 billion broadcasting revenue per season is now over €1 billion more than that of La Liga, its nearest challenger, with Serie A, the Bundesliga, and Ligue 1 trailing far behind.

The windfall is pure profit – straight to the bottom line with no costs attached. The great danger is what the 1990s' Spurs chairman Alan Sugar termed 'the prune-juice effect'; that the money will go straight out again on transfers and wages. The omens are not good. The dramatic fall in revenue during the pandemic – during which time there was no matchday income whatsoever – aggravated the wages-to-turnover ratio in the Premier League from a sustainable 61% to a disconcerting 73%. Spurs' wages-to-turnover ratio jumped from 46% to 57%, the worst for nearly a decade. However, it still remained one of the lowest in the Premier League.

The summer transfer window of 2022 did nothing to allay these fears. By the end of July, over £1 billion had been paid out on transfers, with wages exemplified by the reported £375,000 a week Manchester City were paying to 21-year-old Erling Haaland. The enormous salary was 'compensation' for his buyout clause from Borussia Dortmund being 'only £51 million'. For the world's best players seeking the highest wages, only Qatari-owned Paris St. Germain – able to retain its trio of high earners Lionel Messi, Neymar, and Kylian Mbappe – rivalled the Premier League.

So, with £80 million spent and six new signings, there was an unaccustomed mood of optimism in London N17 as the season hove into view. However, maybe due to the summer heat, maybe the prospect of a season crammed into two halves to accommodate the absurdity of the Qatar World Cup, or perhaps just the familiar nagging doubt that it's the hope that does for you, the optimism was soon tempered by harsh realities. Because, of course, and once again before a ball was kicked, Spurs 'needed' to win a trophy. Now more than ever. Alone among the self-styled Big Six, the club had won nothing for 14 years. And the larger that timespan became, the more the question would be asked about whether Spurs really was a top football club or just an exceptional sporting enterprise.

Winning the League Cup would break the drought, but that would not bring much prestige. The FA Cup would be something more, but the competition was not what it was. All the same, for Spurs, an FA Cup win will always be special because of the relationship the club has had with that competition ever since it became the first – *and still the only* – non-league team to win it all the way back in 1901. Nevertheless, the brutal reality of modern football, aided – it must be said – by some spectacularly careless stewardship of the world's oldest club knockout competition by the FA, dictates that a victorious FA Cup run is only what might be expected of a Big Six club.

These days it is only the Premier League or the Champions League that can put you at the summit. Of the two competitions, the Premier League appeared the more likely, if distant, prospect. Spurs had only to overtake the three teams who finished above them in 2021/2022 – Manchester City and Liverpool, who were 22 and 21 points respectively ahead of them in the final table, and Chelsea, to whom they meekly surrendered four times during the course of the previous season without scoring a single goal. Arsenal's acquisition of Manchester City old boys Gabriel Jesus and Oleksandr Zinchenko meant they could not easily be dismissed, and Manchester United surely could not underperform so spectacularly again.

To work 'in old money' and recognise that the top division was relevant for well over a century before the Premier League came along, a third league title would put Spurs on a par with Huddersfield Town. Emulating them would be a stupendous achievement. To provide more perspective, if Spurs fail to win the league this season, then the club will have gone the entire second half of the English league's existence without being champions. True, a single Premier League title would put Spurs on equal terms with Blackburn (1995), Leicester (2016), and Liverpool (2020), but with the latter, you would need to factor in their six European Cups/Champions Leagues. Spurs are still trying for their first.

Fings ain't wot they used to be. It's a sad fact of the modern game that even gaining a trophy is not what it was. It really wasn't that long ago that securing one of the four prizes on offer in any season was significant in its own right – and the reason was their scarcity value. Now, success is measured in multipacks. One trophy is no longer truly meaningful. It has to be part of a double or treble or quadruple. When only a handful of clubs contend every competition year after year, the scarcity value is diminished, and mission accomplished has to come from something more, some elevation of a simple victory to something grander.

It would be too easy, a little trite even, to say that football fans have become spoiled. Or, to be more specific, that the fans of the top clubs have. When the game is being run by those at the top for the express purpose of ensuring that they stay at the top, then the lack of variety in the list of winners is inevitable. If Spurs did win the Premier League or the Champions League, it might be the start of something. But it could also be seen as the least that needed to happen, or something expected under the laws of probability.

The story of the run to the Champions League final in 2019 highlighted the character of the team and the manager and the connection it had built with the fans. A Spurs win would have shown it was still possible to prevail in the old way, to beat the system by building a team and applying a force of personality that could really mark out success as special rather than securing it simply by spending the most money and acquiring the biggest names. Success is so much more memorable when it comes as the culmination of a tumultuous journey that has taken the fans along with it.

Antonio Conte could be the man to take the club and its fans on the journey of a lifetime. However, he's one of the modern breed of manager who tries his hand at the best teams in turn. Whatever happens, it is hard to see him still at Spurs in two or three years. He is unlikely to follow the example of Jürgen Klopp, who gave himself five years to acquire a trophy for Liverpool and delivered the Champions League after three.

It is hard to imagine Conte building a dynasty. With the notable exceptions of Klopp, and Pep Guardiola at Manchester City, many of the top managers don't work like that any more. You can have all the money in the world, a portfolio as long as both arms and not put a foot wrong, and still be told it's time to move on… just as successive Real Madrid coaches or Chelsea managers under Roman Abramovich had. The aim is to win everything all the time, to dominate competition by destroying competition. Win the treble. Win the double double. Win three in a row. Win 18 league titles or six European cups! English teams have been there and done that. What's next?

The 2022/23 season could end by Spurs opening a new chapter in the club's history. That would be a nice story, albeit a short one. It would need a longer tale to convincingly make the case that Spurs were firmly back at the top table where they haven't been for over 60 years.

But you've got to start somewhere. And Conte's Spurs were about to get started.

3. WHEN SATURDAY COMES

Nine hundred and seventy-three days since they had last kicked off on an ordinary Saturday afternoon at 3pm, Tottenham Hotspur began the 2022/23 season on the 6th of August at home against Southampton.

Playing in Europe ensures fixtures are moved so that the most successful teams – those that play on Tuesdays and Wednesdays – have sufficient time to recover from and prepare for the rigours of the Premier League and the Champions League. Since 2020, Tottenham's participation in second and third-tier European competitions meant they played on Thursdays, with domestic duties invariably taking place on Sundays. With the demands of television, Premier League games were now scheduled across a potential nine time-slots across a week, including Saturday kick-offs at 12.30pm, 5.30pm and 7.45pm. As such, the likelihood of a Saturday 3pm kick-off was a rarity.

The rhythms and routines that embedded Saturday afternoon so deeply into the collective consciousness of Britain are being eroded and replaced by a constant stream of televised product to a global audience. While it is impossible not to be impressed by the Premier League's commercial success – its revenue is almost double that of the Bundesliga and La Liga – further thought raises the question of whether the awareness of the price it can command is matched by an understanding of what contributes to its value.

Football, in Britain, has long been the national sport; its current popularity attracting – in particular – young, free spenders whom commercial companies prize the most. The game provides the raw fuel for Sky's phenomenal success, shifting what was once an ailing satellite punt into a global behemoth. And Sky changed the way that football was financed, presented, and even played, taking the live event watched by thousands and transforming it into a televisual spectacular watched by millions across the world. The biggest corporations now pay large sums to be associated with the Premier League. Even the newer internet and social media giants have joined the growing list of suitors for the competition.

Saturday 3pm was when football traditionally happened. It was easier for people to make it a part of their routine – to plan and enjoy. There were no last-minute changes, no kick-off times moved due to television coverage, no movement to slots that meant the game finished long after the last train left, or involved setting off at ridiculous o'clock to make kick-off. There were few re-arrangements because another team's schedule had been affected by another competition, so that the game you were interested in had to move. Nowadays, if going to the match is to become a regular pursuit, the dedicated fan has to make supporting their team almost a career choice. It requires lots of planning, the ability to be able to alter arrangements at the last minute, plus a lot of time and a lot of money, all of which needs to happen around a pretty well-paid job.

But while those fans who attend games are a minority, they matter. That's something; even the Premier League broke its embrace of the freest of free markets when it introduced a £30 price cap on away tickets (although many clubs have steadily chipped away at the principle ever since it was introduced by withdrawing concessionary pricing and reducing the number of available tickets). Like extras on a film set, fans help create the atmosphere that is such an integral part of the broadcast product (no broadcaster would stump up the lofty rights fee if Spurs hosted Arsenal in a half-empty stadium) and while the suggestion that the football bubble is going to burst looks far off the mark, there is a growing sense of discontent. All the same, Premier League stadia are fuller than ever, filling over 95% capacity in season 2021/22, despite ticket prices reaching astronomic levels. Eleven of the 20 Premier League clubs have raised their prices for 2022/23, with the average most-expensive adult season ticket costing £946. The cheapest is a mere £420, at Crystal Palace, with the £927 at Arsenal the most expensive of the cheapest prices for a season ticket. Nevertheless, there is a waiting list of thousands for most clubs, so it's not surprising that they take a *laissez-faire* attitude towards supporters.

*

The new season had brought with it news that the use of pyrotechnics and supporter encroachment on the pitch would be cracked down on, and while most fans – and notably the Football Supporters' Association (FSA) – backed the move, the thought that football was always more eager to pursue punitive measures against supporters than to act in a way that benefited them, was never too far away.

A rational observer would ask why customers who are treated so badly would keep going back for more, but football's pull so often defies rational analysis. Even so, one has to wonder how much longer it will be before there is some sea-change, before going to the match becomes just another expensive leisure choice. There's no doubt the size of the audience will be huge for a long time yet, but the nature and composition of that audience is important, and an increasing number of factors – now including the most serious cost-of-living crisis in decades – are pulling at the seams. When football stops being the most important of the unimportant things, when it loses its special connection with the collective consciousness, how valuable will it be?

On a sun-drenched opening Saturday in London N17, though, as 3pm approached, any sense of foreboding or indeed any philosophical questioning of the state of the game seemed far removed. The bars and restaurants of the billion-pound Tottenham Hotspur Stadium were packed; tickets for the first three home games were already sold out; the grass was pristine; and expectation among the 61,732 patrons was high.

Inevitably, opponents Southampton scored first. James Ward-Prowse took advantage of some lax defending to volley the ball into the turf and past Hugo Lloris after just 12 minutes. Conte's 3-4-3 starting line-up had contained no surprises, with new signings either not quite match fit or, in Richarlison's case, suspended. The words 'here we go again' were not far from many Spurs fans' lips.

However, the early shock sparked the white shirts into life, producing a reaction in which they displayed the movement and ambition that had been so often absent since the departure of Mauricio Pochettino (albeit against opponents that made it easy at times). Ryan Sessegnon, showing signs of at last fulfilling his undoubted promise, headed Spurs level from a perfect Dejan Kulusevski cross and, on 30 minutes, Eric Dier's clever stooping header put the hosts ahead.

After the break, it was Sessegnon impressing again when finding the net, but the effort was ruled out for offside. Still, Spurs came forward, the pressure forcing Saints' defender Mohammed Salisu to turn an Emerson Royal cross into his own net for one of the most inept own goals witnessed in a long while. To cap it off, the consistently impressive Kulusevski cut in to curve a peach of a shot into the far corner.

Tottenham Hotspur had made hay while the sun shone, with a 4-1 opening day win!

*

Tottenham's next game provided an early opportunity to put some assumptions to the test. With the new arrivals – none of whom made the starting line-up for the opening fixture – increasing the pressure for places, expectations were higher than hitherto against Chelsea. The West London side was under new ownership after Russian oligarch Roman Abramovich had been sanctioned and forced to sell following his country's invasion of Ukraine. There have always been rich men in football, but no one had spent so much, so quickly, and to such effect as Abramovich. His lavish spending of £2 billion during his tenure seemed destined to give his club dominance of the game for years to come. It also bestowed standing and respectability on the owner, and in so doing alerted others as to what could be achieved through the successful stewardship of an English Premier League club.

Arguably, without Abramovich blazing the trail, the current owners of the majority of Premier League clubs would not be in place. Now, Manchester City had put Chelsea in the shade with a dose of their own medicine, and in doing so raised a fundamental question about the economic reality of modern football. To win the Premier League, was it now only possible with the unlimited resources that nation-states could provide? For all the fine words about financial fair play and sporting integrity, it seemed that unlimited amounts of money could be poured into a club, with the aid of some suitably complex financial engineering – the sort that big money could buy.

The Premier League's main concern was that the product's image wasn't sullied, but its view of reputational damage was not shared far outside its own ranks. It had, for example, declared itself happy that Newcastle United's new owners were not owned by a nation-state but by a sovereign investment fund, which was perfectly acceptable. For most other people, the clue was in the name. The Premier League's stance allowed those inconvenient questions about human rights to be batted away – a precedent already set twice with Manchester City. That absolute need to avoid any nastiness had meant the question of how Abramovich had obtained his money was never really considered, with the outcome that the spend, spend, spend that had elevated that club to its current position would not be addressed. The owner had to go because even the UK government was cutting links with Russian investors, but the chief objective appeared to be that new owners could come in as seamlessly as possible. No matter that Chelsea's skewing of the game's finances had given it, along with one or two others, what could be construed as an unfair competitive advantage and fuelled a financial madhouse in which clubs were incentivised to take unwise risks just to keep up. Chelsea would now need to be run as a business. The Todd Boelhy consortium was not short of money, but it wouldn't be able to write off £1.4 billion of debt, as Abramovich had done.

The new Chelsea regime had replaced many senior figures, including the respected Sporting Director Petr Cech, and Marina Granovskaia, who had been widely credited as the key figure in the club's transfer activities. The result had been the reported pursuit of a lengthy list of players the Blues had failed to sign – a story not unfamiliar to Spurs fans. Nevertheless, Boelhy spent freely, £175 million on the likes of Raheem Sterling from Manchester City and Marc Cucurella from Brighton, and he had yet to close his chequebook.

So, this early-season battle at Stamford Bridge pitted two rivals at a crossroads. Would the relative calm and organisation at Spurs give them the edge over a nemesis in transition? Or would the story be the same – as it had so often been in the recent past – with Chelsea exposing just how far short Spurs were?

The verdict after a pulsating encounter was that Spurs were not as good, and Chelsea weren't as bad, as many thought they might be. Chelsea flooded the midfield and stopped Spurs flowing. They were defiant where the visitors were lacklustre, and they were sharper in front of goal. But a late, late disputed headed equaliser from Harry Kane enabled Spurs to come away with a point from a 2-2 draw. It was the type of match they would have lost without Antonio Conte. (The cover of *The Times* football supplement *The Game* accompanied a picture of Kane's goal with the caption 'Not so Spursy[3] any more'). Conte had made them stronger, tougher, with more choices from the bench to make a difference as he did with his telling use of Ivan Perišić, Yves Bissouma, and Richarlison.

However, it was the events following the final whistle, and the intense celebrations as the Spurs players dived into the front rows of the away section, that dominated the post-match discussion. Chelsea manager Thomas Tuchel, incensed that fouls by Rodrigo Bentancur and Cristian Romero which preceded both equalisers had gone unnoticed, gripped Conte's hand for the customary post-match handshake but did not let go as his opposite number attempted to walk away. Conte was jerked backwards, and within seconds a mass of players, squad members, officials and staff were involved in an unseemly melee.

---

[3] A pejorative term used by opponents alluding to Spurs' expected typical underperformance. (Yet all teams disappoint but are not habitually categorised in the same negative way.)

Tuchel attempted to explain his own actions after the game by saying, 'I thought when you shake hands you looked in each other's eyes. He had a different opinion.' Conte refused to get drawn in as the post-match controversy swirled.

In the aftermath, the 'something must be done' stage was swiftly reached. Criticise the game's authorities all you want for turning a blind eye to dodgy owners, ceding control of kick-off times to broadcasters and competitive balance to foreign parties, and allowing some fundamental traditions to be undermined, but when a post-match spat happens, they are down on it like a ton of bricks. Both managers were given red cards and fined.

*

At home to Wolverhampton Wanderers the following weekend, Spurs once again struggled against a side that crowded the midfield. Wolves were smart and could consider themselves unlucky to come away with nothing after Spurs took the three points thanks to a Harry Kane goal that took him to 250 for his club. It was an achievement that underlined the sheer consistency and quality of a player still, incredibly, not seen by a significant section of the wider football public as one of the contemporary greats.

The goal came courtesy of Perišić, who cleverly flicked back a header from a corner to set up Kane. It was the third of three goals scored from set pieces, a dramatic improvement on the meagre eight managed during the whole of the previous season. It exemplified the meticulous attention to detail of Conte's assistant, Gianni Vio. He analyses a multitude of set piece routines in order to establish the manoeuvres that exploit the strengths of Spurs' personnel and expose any fallibility in the opposition ranks.

Perišić was the first of the summer signings to start, replacing Sessegnon as left wing-back. Richarlison came on and generally made a nuisance of himself. His energy and impact also highlighted the lean period Son Heung-Min is going through. Sonny is a popular figure, and there was no sustained criticism or evidence of the crowd getting on his back, just recognition that sometimes a change is as good as a rest.

Of the other signings, little was being seen. Conte's starting line-up and tactics were firmly set, and the coach's style is to stick with his judgement. He was dismissive of calls to bring the new blood in early, saying he could not understand how people expected them to immediately pick up the systems and shapes required to successfully compete at this level.

*

August Bank Holiday weekend brought a return to the City Ground to play newly-promoted Nottingham Forest. It was a fixture that brought back memories of a different age, when the two teams seemed fated to play each other in multiple competitions over many seasons in the late 1980s and early 1990s. Forest, then, were still a force under the legendary Brian Clough, although his redoubtable coaching powers were on the wane. The culmination of the confrontations came in the 1991 FA Cup Final, when Terry Venables's Spurs denied Clough the last chance to win the only domestic trophy he had never lifted.

Since then, fortunes had diverged. Forest had been a founder member of the Premier League, but dropped out in 1999. It had taken two decades to return, and the club were now relative minnows among the powerhouses of the elite flight. Even so, they had won the League championship more recently than Spurs and, more significantly, had won two European Cups to Spurs' none, giving them a place in football's hierarchy that Spurs could only dream about.

Maybe Spurs presumed Forest's pedigree and felt justified in announcing the pricing of the opening Champions League game (against Olympique Marseille on the 7th of September) at the second-highest tariff of the three it uses for Premier League games. After all, this was the Champions League, and Marseille were 'a big name' weren't they? The draw had been kind to Spurs, with the French side completing a trio of opponents that included Eintracht Frankfurt and Sporting Lisbon. No team reaches the competition without talent, but these clubs were not Europe's giants. If Category B ticketing was imposed for this fixture, would it be the case for the other group games? And what would it mean if qualification for the knockout stages was achieved?

The club had already sold out its first four home games, and brought forward on-sale dates so that tickets for the first six were available. The six-week break to accommodate the Qatar World Cup meant many more early-season games – 16 in the Premier League alone – and thus much more expense for fans. For those dedicated to following the team home and away, a considerable investment was required. The club could, as it had before, have put a package of three Champions League home tickets on sale at a discount in return for a commitment to all three. It could have used the fact that the stadium generates £5 million+ a game to offset the financial burden on fans who were dealing with the worst cost-of-living crisis in decades. It chose not to, opting for prices that were far higher than the European Champions of 2021 and London neighbours Chelsea were charging. One suspected, however, that even in what can, at times, be the most detached of boardrooms, there was an inkling that this was a difficult choice, as the club was reticent about announcing its policy. So those fans who were registered for the club's automatic ticket allocation scheme had to check their bank balances to find out what they had been charged.

Something had to give and it did, with the club announcing – one week after the Marseille tickets went on sale – that 'Season Ticket holders can now buy up to four guest tickets'. In other words, sales were not going as well as anticipated. But the guest ticket offer poured salt on the wound. Season ticket holders who couldn't attend had been told they would not be able to use the popular ticket share scheme. This had been set up to enable fans to pass tickets they could not use to fellow fans on the club's database, therefore eliminating a source of touting and providing an opportunity to share tickets with friends and family. The problem with ticket share, though, is that it doesn't generate extra income, whereas giving people the chance to buy more tickets does. So much for the security concerns used to justify not operating the ticket share scheme.

A pulsating encounter at Forest's City Ground saw Spurs continue their unbeaten run with a victory courtesy of a brace from Kane – even though he missed his first penalty after 18 consecutive successful Premier League strikes. Once again, though, Spurs struggled to show any encouraging signs that they had solved the problem of how to break down defences marshalled behind a plan to crowd out the middle and disrupt supply lines to the opposition forwards.

Musing on what to make of it all, Alan Fisher, whose *Tottenham On My Mind* blog is a mature and insightful outpost of common sense in a sea of mundane online comment, summed up the unease felt by Spurs fans whose early optimism was suffering as familiar doubts tapped them on the shoulder. 'Conte has unshakeable confidence in his system and in his defenders to implement it', he wrote. 'I'm a Spurs fan. I expect things not to turn out as we expect or hope.'

The Guardian's Jonathan Liew's view was that Spurs 'are not yet good enough or organised enough to control games high up the pitch or starve opponents of possession.' His conclusion summed up the first four games of the campaign. 'Tottenham, improbably, are third in the Premier League. Nobody really knows what it means yet.'

Controversy, once more, was the order of the day's post-match debate. Richarlison had indulged in a bout of 'keepy-uppie' late on as Spurs defended their lead – and had been cleaned out by Forest's Brennan Johnson for his troubles. This gave assorted rent-a-quote ex-pros plenty to get stuck into. Jamie Carragher took the time to inform the public that actions such as Richarlison's 'wind me up' and said the player was 'taking the p***', while Dietmar Hamman said the Spurs man, 'should have been booked for unsportsmanlike conduct'. Fisher had the measure of it. 'Richarlison did 'keepie-uppies' and took the whatsit – I laughed. He got done – I laughed. That's what should have happened. But then I don't earn a living from keeping a non-debate going incessantly.'

*

The month ended with a trip across town. West Ham had been in poor form, and so it was inevitable they would put in their best performance to date against Spurs, just as Chelsea had a couple of weeks before. As one fan remarked in the run-up to the game: 'If you told West Ham and Chelsea they were playing us in every game, they would finish first and second every season.'

And so it proved, with wobbles from Hugo Lloris and an unusual unprofessional lapse in concentration by Pierre-Emile Højbjerg helping West Ham take a deserved point after an own goal had put the visitors in front. Bissouma started, but looked somewhat forlorn – perhaps underlining Conte's point about new players and established systems.

The following day, the 1st of September, saw the end of the transfer window. This time, there was no Tottenham Hotspur-related drama as the business had been completed early on. But the club still hadn't landed the left-sided central defender rumoured to have been sought, nor had it addressed the right wing-back problem. Despite the optimism, the familiar doubts and rumbles of discontent remained. Conte subsequently gave an interview in which he enigmatically noted, 'We did what the club could do'. He added there was still 'too much distance' to the top teams and that 'to be competitive and to be a title contender', the club would need 'at least three windows'. One down, two to go?

To say there was a gap between most teams and the pundits' favourites for the title, Manchester City and Liverpool, was hardly a revelation. However, was it wise to imply 'We're not good enough' so early in proceedings? Conte is a smart operator with a voracious appetite for victory, so his every statement is examined for evidence of how he may be challenging the board to prioritise the football rather than the business.

For Spurs, the transfer window looked to have been one of the club's better ones. Its net spend, though, of £113 million was only the sixth-highest in a staggering £1.91 billion splurged by Premier League clubs, a year-to-year rise of 67% more than the *combined* outlay of La Liga,[4] the Bundesliga, Serie

---

[4] The one club to match the leading Premier League spenders was Barcelona. When Joan Laporta assumed the presidency of Barcelona in March 2021, he inherited a debt of over €1 billion courtesy of Lionel Messi's wages of more than €1 million a week and those of Antoine Griezmann, Phillipe Coutinho and Ousmane Dembele whose acquisitions alone cost just shy of €400 million. Determined to remain competitive, drastic action was a prerequisite. Messi and Griezmann left and Dembele was re-signed on a reduced salary. However, in order to replenish the

A, and Ligue 1. An example of the discrepancy was that newly promoted Nottingham Forest would receive, wherever it finished in the table, more money from domestic broadcast rights than Bayern Munich. Flushed with this newly acquired wealth, the ambitious owner, Evangelos Marinakis, proceeded to underwrite a net spend of £128 million in an attempt to preserve the club's fresh status.

For Nottingham Forest, success means survival; for others, there are loftier ambitions such as European competition, but all 20 members of the select Premier League fraternity have to have their version of success. And the only way to secure it is through extravagant outlay on players' wages and transfers. With transfer spending amortised over the length of a player's contract – e.g., in a purchase of £80 million with a four-year contract, only £20 million is accountable in that year's financial

---

squad, millions more was required. The money arrived courtesy of a 25% sale of the club's broadcast revenues from La Liga for the next 25 years to Sixth Street, a US-based investment company. A section of the merchandising operation was also sold and a stadium naming rights deal was made with Spotify. So, Robert Lewandowski arrived from Bayern Munich, Raphinha from Leeds, and Jules Koundé from Sevilla with Laporta's justification, 'Our supporters are used to and deserve a competitive team.'

statement – there was no brake on the desire to spend. Further, with new owners anxious to make their mark, and only four places available for the bonanza of the Champions League, and with the Premier League set to comply with UEFA's new regulations stipulating a spending limit of 70% of revenue, clubs spent as they did simply because they could afford to do so. Back in May 2022, former Arsenal Chief Executive Ivan Gazidis, now in a similar role at AC Milan, warned, 'The reality is the Premier League is the Super League. The rest of European football will not be able to just accept that, and allow the Premier League to have the global landscape to itself.'

With the first round in the group stages of the Champions League starting on the 6th of September, any response to the dominance of the Premier League is likely to be postponed until after the World Cup ends on the 18th of December, but the European Super League will then surely come back on the agenda, perhaps initially in a continental format with the exclusion of the English Big Six. A question of waiting to see how the ball bounces...

4. THE EUROPEAN QUESTION

September would see Spurs once more enter the stage upon which Bill Nicholson, the most successful manager in their history, said they must be present or *they were nothing* – Europe.

Nowadays, it is the Champions League – not just any old European competition – that the self-respecting model of a major modern football club had to qualify for. Bill also talked about setting sights high, 'so that even in failure there is an echo of glory.' But, while echoes of glory may be welcome, it is cash in the coffers that is indispensable. And, aside from the Premier League, nothing generates cash like the Champions League.

Merely being in the group stages of the competition guarantees a club €15.64 million, with €2.8 million given for each win and €930,000 for a draw. Qualification for the knockout stage brings in €9.6 million, with €85.14 million available to the clubs that reach the final. To this can be added much more in the form of the shares of the television pool (the value of the country's broadcast rights agreement). This is divided up according to the domestic league position (by finishing fourth, Spurs received only 10% compared to champions Manchester City's 40%), co-efficient rankings from past performances, and how well their compatriots perform. So, the top earner would be the champion from the most lucrative television market – England or Germany – whose fellow clubs were eliminated early on. When Spurs reached the Final in 2019, the club earned €102 million, which was topped up by many more millions from matchday and commercial revenues.

Of course, the prestige of winning the Champions League is still hugely significant. But the cold economic reality for Spurs is that with such stupendous sums on offer, being in the competition year after year, with only four places available to share among the Big Six, is a vital prerequisite in order to put more and more distance between themselves and the other Champions League hopefuls. That's why former Arsenal manager, Arsène Wenger, called the fourth and last qualifying place for Premier League clubs, 'The first trophy'. He proceeded to qualify for 16 successive years, to the undoubted delight of the owner for whom the bottom line appeared to be of paramount concern. Supporters, however, were often dismayed as their team frequently fell at the first knockout hurdle.

The evolution of the Champions League from the original European Cup is a history of modern football's attempts to balance the jeopardy of sport with the certainty a business requires. And the 2022/23 tournament would be the last before yet another change in the format (to appease the big clubs, naturally) takes the competition even further away from its roots. The 2023/24 season will see the introduction of four more teams, taking the number of participants in the group stage from 32 to 36, thereby increasing the number of games. So much for protestations about overcrowded calendars.

It's all a long way from 1954, when the seeds of the competition were sown. The previous year, England, the self-proclaimed masters of the game, were humbled 6-3 by the Magical Magyars of Hungary at Wembley. It was a seismic shock to the system that made the more progressive-minded managers and coaches realise that their teams needed to test themselves against the best in Europe, if they were not to fall further behind.

A year previously, in June 1953, the coronation of Queen Elizabeth II was watched by an estimated television audience of 27 million out of a UK population of 51 million, ushering in the television age. In anticipation of the big day, thousands of television sets were bought or rented, laying the foundation for the big events of the national game to benefit.

Football was propelled centre stage by the FA Cup Final in the month before the coronation. The game was billed as the last chance for 38-year-old Blackpool and England winger Stanley Matthews to earn a winner's medal. In a pulsating encounter, Bolton Wanderers were defeated 4-3 with Matthews laying on the winning goal in the closing minutes. (The match was subsequently known as 'The

Matthews Final' even though his teammate, Stan Mortensen, scored a hat-trick.) An estimated 10 million viewers watched the spectacular and convinced the BBC that football's special events were worth televising. So, the following year, when Wolverhampton Wanderers – the English champions – hosted two friendlies under floodlights, they were broadcast live at peak time. At the same time, the appeal of football on TV was being noticed across Europe as mass communication began to make the world a smaller place.

In November 1954, Wolves demolished Spartak Moscow 4-0. A month later, they beat Hungarian champions Honvéd – including seven players who had featured in the Wembley victory – 3-2. Coming six months after Hungary had humiliated England once more (this time with a 7-1 thrashing in Budapest), the victories prompted great delight. The *Daily Mail* pronounced Wolves, 'Champions of the World' but, in what would not be the last time a *Daily Mail* headline would go down badly in Europe, Gabriel Hanot,[5] the editor of the French sports newspaper *L'Equipe*, was quick to counter. 'Before

---

[5] Gabriel Hanot was a France international player and manager (he fired himself when he felt he had fallen short in his duties). As well as being one of the founders of the European Cup, he was also responsible for the Ballon D'Or. One of a rare species, a true football visionary.

we declare that Wolverhampton are invincible, let them go to Moscow and Budapest', he wrote. 'A club world championship, or at least a European one… should be launched.'

Together with his colleague, Jacques Ferran, Hanot canvassed European champions, and petitioned UEFA, and in 1955 it was agreed that a 16-team cup competition would be launched. The English FA, supported by the Football League, displayed the lack of foresight and humility that characterised their administrations and refused to have anything to do with such distractions from the all-important domestic game. Chelsea, the English champions, were forbidden to participate. It was hard not to detect a whiff of disdain for a concept as unsavoury as English football having to prove itself in a continental competition that was not of its making. The English authorities had, after all, declined to participate in the first three World Cups before belatedly making a disastrous appearance in 1950.

The rest, as they say, is history and English clubs were not to be left behind – although only due to the foresight of managers such as Matt Busby, who ignored the FA's edict not to take part. The European Cup quickly established itself as the ultimate stage; its allure made all the more relevant by the fact that – after initial compromises to enable the event to get up and running – only the champions of UEFA's member associations were allowed to compete.

When Real Madrid took the first five trophies back-to-back, the last in 1960 in a 7-3 demolition of Eintracht Frankfurt in front of 134,000 at Hampden Park (enthralling millions watching on Eurovision); when Bill Nicholson's 'Team of the Century' pitted themselves against Europe's best; when Jock Stein's Celtic in 1967 and Matt Busby's Manchester United the following year became the first British champions; when Rinus Michels and Johan Cruyff's Ajax and Franz Beckenbauer's Bayern Munich took turns to dominate in 1970s; when Liverpool laid the roots of their European tradition and Nottingham Forest astonishingly won twice running, the achievements really resonated. These moments – these treasures – were all the more precious because of their rarity and the widespread acceptance of the European Cup as the pinnacle of club football.

However, the vagaries of chance – that David could beat Goliath – had begun to concern the big clubs and when the 1987 draw pitted the champions of Spain, Real Madrid, against Napoli, the Italian champions, the writing was on the wall. Silvio Berlusconi, the owner of AC Milan, was aghast. 'The European Cup has become an historical anachronism,' he proclaimed. 'It is economic nonsense that a club such as Milan might be eliminated in the first round. It is not modern thinking.'

Berlusconi's subsequent plan, produced for him by the advertising agency Saatchi & Saatchi, was for a

European Super League of 18 clubs selected on criteria of merit, history, and size – thereby focusing on the big clubs in the big television markets. It foreshadowed the cackhanded ESL scheme of 2021.

The threat of a breakaway league forced UEFA to contemplate change which became inevitable as more practical solutions were proposed by Glasgow Rangers. (Rangers had suffered the same fate in the UEFA cup as Napoli, who lost to Real Madrid.) Campbell Ogilvy, the Rangers Secretary, put their case. 'For all clubs of our size, how do we take this forward? Can we get into some sort of structure where we could be guaranteed six games?' he asked. In 1991, after the third Rangers submission, supported by Real Madrid and with Berlusconi's Super League plan hovering in the background, a group stage was added to the European Cup and, in 1992, the competition was rebranded the Champions League. The simple, straightforward knockout formula was consigned to history, replaced by the complicated bureaucracy required to dish out ever-increasing amounts of cash.

UEFA likes to present what it does in terms of fairness. So, in its view, it was fair to give more countries a chance, and fair to do away with the notion that only champions should play in the Champions League. UEFA argued that in order to fulfil the primary objective – deciding Europe's best team – then the fourth-placed English team had just as much right to be considered as the champions of the smaller countries.

As the 2022 campaign began with the habitual glittering, overblown draw 'event' – this time in Istanbul, where the final would be held – it was fanciful to think UEFA might pause to reflect on how shamefully the fans were treated at its showcase final a few months before, at the Stade de France in Paris. Indolent, inefficient policing and stewarding allowed fans to be assaulted and pepper sprayed, with the least of their troubles turning out to be missing a match for which they had paid handsomely. For fans, especially the away ones whose experience of nasty and basic facilities, plus oppressive violent stewarding and policing, was firmly embedded against a backdrop of indifference from the authorities, this shocking treatment was no surprise. What would Gabriel Hanot and Jacques Ferran have made of their noble vision today?

UEFA's bungled organisation in Paris, along with its lack of empathy for the fans, effectively ended its attempts to present itself as the good guy after the ESL debacle. Prompted by supporters' groups, especially those from England, it had taken a strong stance against the rebel alliance. This looked increasingly to have been driven by the realisation that the ESL would have fatally undermined the Champions League, rather than the professed 'concern for the values of the game' that President Aleksander Čeferin had made much of. An opportunity had been spurned to wrest back some power from the mega clubs who were forcing changes. The sense that events were heading towards a different version of a closed pan-European competition staged for the convenience of a select few and a global television audience was always present in the background.

Yet it still mattered that Spurs were back in the Champions League, because being at the top table – however it is laid out – is a minimum requirement. Hopes were high for a memorable adventure, commencing with a European night under the lights – an occasion that has much vibrancy in N17. Moreover, it was a competition in which Antonio Conte needed to prove himself. 'I am sure' he reflected, 'I will win it (as a coach). I won it as a player (with Juventus) and I'll win it as a coach.' But he hadn't come close to realising his ambition so far, achieving a meagre 33% win rate. Indeed, in three of his five Champions League outings, he hadn't even emerged from the group stage. The furthest he had progressed was to the quarter-finals with Juventus. Conte's European record was in stark contrast to his domestic CV, where he had won titles with three different clubs in Italy and England. But Europe is the arena in which the all-time great coaches must succeed.

*

On the first weekend of September, goals in each half from Højbjerg and Kane gave Spurs a deserved 2-1 victory at home over Fulham. With 14 points from six league games safely tucked away, the team should have been in good fettle four days later to welcome Olympique Marseille to the Tottenham Hotspur Stadium. This was the first Champions League outing since the abject loss to RB Leipzig in 2020, a tie which took place against a nagging background of worries about a virus called Covid-19.

Much had happened since then, with a global crisis putting the struggles of football into perspective. Nevertheless, in North London, there had been trials and tribulations aplenty. Manager José Mourinho had been fired; an act of bizarre timing due to his record of winning a trophy at every club he'd managed, and taking place as he prepared his team to contest the League Cup Final! Some thought that he'd polarised the dressing room so badly his sacking was Spurs' best chance of lifting the trophy, but only one man knows precisely why the manager was fired when he was, and that's Daniel Levy. The chairman had pursued Mourinho but then found out when he got what he wanted… that he hadn't wanted what he'd got!

Mourinho's dismissal ushered in yet another period of drift, first under the popular but inexperienced Ryan Mason and then with Nuno Espirito Santo, who could best be described as an available option. Throw in the destabilising saga of Kane apparently trying to engineer a move to Manchester City and it had been anything but a tranquil time. Conte's arrival, though, had dramatically changed the climate, and 10 months on, Spurs were back where they wanted to be. The question was now not one of how far they'd come, but of how far they could go to challenge the kings of Europe.

On the night, the stadium bounced but Spurs didn't, turning in a sluggish display that only delivered when the visitors had a man sent off and the hosts deployed a fourth forward. One of them, Richarlison, who had done everything but score against Fulham, bagged his first goals for the club – a brace of headers. He was serenaded with the latest popular anthem from the stands, an adaptation of an old Manfred Mann hit:

'Doo-wah-diddy, diddy dum, diddy doo;

Tottenham's new Brazilian wearing white and blue;

He looks good;

He looks fine;

Richarlison is on my mind;

And he's Tottenham's number 9'.

Unfortunately, events of a more unsavoury nature off the pitch hogged the post-match headlines as, in the closing minutes of the game, Marseille ultras attempted to break into the home areas of the North Stand. The incident culminated in police being deployed to keep the rival fans apart, but not before fireworks were let off inside the ground.[6]

Despite the disturbances and the somewhat indifferent performance, the home fans went away content with the result. It was noticeable, though, that the crowd of just under 56,000 was around 5,000 short of capacity. The club maintained this was a great show of support at a game for which there had been relatively limited notice. Those who had criticised the pricing policy saw it as proof they had a point.

*

Two days later, on the 8th of September 2022, another event of global proportions once again put football into perspective. The death of Queen Elizabeth II was announced, and the country went into a period of mourning. However, the decision to cancel all games at every level the following weekend made many supporters question whether the authorities' perspective was correct. Other sports had decided to go ahead with their fixtures.

There was widespread approval of a statement from the English Rugby Football Union (RFU) that observed, 'Rugby, at its heart, is about community and bringing people together, in good times and in

---

[6] UEFA fined Marseille €32,500 for 'crowd disturbances, throwing objects and lighting fireworks' and Tottenham €6,000 for 'throwing objects'.

sad. Rugby clubs are a source of strength and support during times of uncertainty and we hope that by enabling games and other rugby activity to go ahead this weekend, with families and friends congregating, it will help us all to unite at this time of national mourning.'

The same sentiment applied to football, of course; so why were supporters faced with a blank weekend? Naturally, there was a dilemma to be faced. Go ahead and the chances were – at Premier League level at least – there would have been accusations of being disrespectful and focusing solely on money. Don't go ahead and the risk was you'd be criticised for not giving supporters a chance to pay their respects.

Much as the RFU's stance was praised, the Premier League, as the pinnacle of the national sport, had an especially tough choice to make. Add in the reticence of the government – whose shelf life at the time was being compared to that of a lettuce in a tabloid live-streaming stunt – to issue clear advice, and it's not hard to sympathise with the quandary that faced the football authorities.

Spurs, then, did not face Manchester City in a top-of-the-table clash. Instead, they next ran out in Lisbon against Sporting on Champions League matchday two, on the 13th of September, having had the luxury of selecting from a first-choice squad after their free weekend.

Despite the advantages they took into the game, with Richarlison starting in place of Kulusevski rather than the off-key Son, Spurs laboured once again. It appeared they were trying not to lose rather than to win. Former Spur (though he only made one substitute appearance for the first team in a League Cup tie) Marcus Edwards was outstanding for Sporting, and if he had been able to positively conclude his Messi-like dribble, it would have been one of the goals of the season. His skill brought to mind Mauricio Pochettino's comparison with the Argentine maestro. On the night, Edwards outshone the former Sporting home-grown favourite Eric Dier and indeed everyone else on the pitch.

With the final whistle about to be blown, the mundane encounter was set to be described as 'the type of away performance you sometimes need in Europe'. As indeed it was for 89 minutes. Unfortunately for Spurs, football matches last for 90 minutes plus injury time, and two goals were conceded in the final minute, one due to some dreadful defending from Emerson Royal. The dereliction of duty signalled Spurs' first defeat of the season and cost the club the competition's draw bonus of a cool €930,000.

The fans, kept behind for some time after the whistle, now had the usual tale to tell of a great trip spoiled by the football. Lisbon is a lovely city, but the pleasures of foreign travel are off-limits when you go to a Champions League game. The visiting contingent swapped stories of poor treatment, worse views, long queues for water, and all the other niceties served up by the club competition, which claims to feature 'The best of the best on the ultimate stage'.

The abject loss, along with the prospect of having to play twice a week till the break for the World Cup in November, ensured that there would be a shake-up in selection. Conte reiterated his warning that 'All the players have to accept the rotation, especially up front where we have four players' (Kane, Son, Richarlison and Kulusevski).

With no goals in eight games, Son appeared first in line for the substitute role. He had endured similar barren scoring runs before, having started 2018 by finding the net in only his tenth outing. Perhaps he had created the issue himself by performing beyond expectation with 12 goals in the final ten games of the previous season. Now, for the first time in his Spurs career, his starting place was under threat. But with Kane seemingly undroppable and with Richarlison's two goals and two assists in his last four games, Kulusevski – though outstanding since coming into the team – was the one who had been sacrificed. Nonetheless, Kulusevski continued to be effective as a substitute. In fact, after his late entry at 72 minutes against Sporting, he and Richarlison were more of a threat than either Kane or Son had been.

*

The following weekend brought Leicester City, surprise occupants of the bottom spot in the table, to North London and the opportunity for Spurs fans to belatedly pay their respects to The Queen. The club produced a classy and respectful cover for the match programme, black and white with gold print and a picture of Danny Blanchflower receiving the FA Cup from Her Majesty. The minute's silence before kick-off was disappointingly observed by a minority, although the crowd did self-police the miscreants who preferred the sound of their own voices, and applause on 70 minutes to commemorate her reign rounded off the paying of respect.

The big news was that Son had been dropped, but still the team was not quite clicking into gear. The match itself was a topsy-turvy cracker with both sides looking vulnerable. The visitors went ahead as early as the sixth minute, but Spurs soon clawed one back through Kane, scoring his sixth of the season, and then took the lead through Højbjerg before Leicester hit back with an equaliser. They had more possession with four and sometimes five going forward. Then Rodrigo Bentancur stole the ball from a dallying Ndidi and coolly put Spurs ahead to take the wind out of their sails.

With half an hour to go, Son came on for Richarlison to a rapturous reception, whilst Yves Bissouma replaced Kulusveski in a midfield 3-5-2 formation. After 664 minutes without a goal, Son took precisely 13 minutes to score three. In the 73rd minute, he cut inside and curled an absolute beauty of a right-footer from 25 yards into the net. He simply walked across to face the crowd in the south-west corner of the ground and stood, as if to say, 'There you go, I'm back, sorry for the break in service'. Eleven minutes later, he recreated the strike, but this time curling it in with his left, to put Spurs 5-2 up, and minutes later slid the ball past Leicester keeper Danny Ward to secure his hat-trick. The emotion was put on hold once again by the Video Assistant Referee (VAR)[7] sucking joy and spontaneity out of the moment, but this time also proving its worth by showing the officials had wrongly ruled the goal out for offside.

Spurs were somewhat flattered by the 6-2 final score, but they had shown evidence of moving up a gear, and the day was all about Son's return to form. He is hugely popular with teammates, staff, and fans alike, and his reaction to being dropped underlined just why. No histrionics, no selective leaks to the press, just a calm acceptance of his manager's decision and then a steely determination to re-assert himself when given the chance.

---

[7] VAR was added to the laws of the game in 2018. By use of video replays scrutinised by a referee, its purpose is to assist the on-field referee to avoid 'clear and obvious errors' and 'serious missed incidents'.

The match demonstrated the benefits of competition for the striking roles. 'We have just started but if the players want to play for something important, to lift a trophy, they have to understand this' [rotation], Conte told *The Athletic*. 'Otherwise they continue to play every game but they don't win anything… If you want to stay in a team with ambition, you have to accept this type of situation. Otherwise you go to a medium team, and then you are sure you will play every game and then it will be very difficult to lift a trophy in this way.'

So, the acid test for Antonio Conte is to select the right team, especially his strikers, at the right time. His choices could define Spurs' season. There would be fewer tests more charged than the next game…

5. THE OTHER LOT

The nerves kick in as soon as you wake up.

North London Derby day is eagerly anticipated but fractiously endured every year. Fans wouldn't do without it, but enjoyment doesn't seem to be the appropriate word to describe the day – unless your team comes out on top.

It still matters so much.

The Cambridge Dictionary defines a derby as 'a sports competition, especially a game of football, between two teams from the same city or area'. Some of the most famous football derbies draw their intensity from religious, political, or class divisions, but Spurs v Arsenal is fuelled *more than anything else* by intense irritation. Spurs fans are always ready to point out that Arsenal are really a south London club. Arsenal fans insist Spurs are from Middlesex, which isn't really London.

The status of this derby has been questioned by observers picking up on what they see as the lack of any true significance beyond parochial rivalry. Since the formation of the Premier League in 1992, there has been a relative change in the fortunes of the two clubs. It is a competition which they both were prime movers in creating, but which Arsenal have used as a springboard to become a modern super club, securing their second Double in 1998 – years before Spurs got their act together to even contend. Arsenal fans liked to claim that the derby no longer mattered. Spurs, they insisted, weren't their true rivals – Manchester United and Barcelona were. But they weren't really convincing themselves. The rivalry not only endures but has intensified as both clubs battle for the cherished Champions League place while continuing to glower at each other from their relative positions at each end of the Seven Sisters Road.

London's workplaces and gathering points and its immediate environs still buzz with tension in the lead-up to derby day. No piece of one-upmanship is ignored, no quip goes unparried. Spurs fans remind their Arsenal neighbours that they are the only team to be present in the top division without achieving that status on merit. Arsenal fans retort that they have won the League twice on their neighbour's ground. And so on and so forth.

The absence of the kind of divisive political and religious edges to other derbies notwithstanding, Spurs and Arsenal arguably have the most complex of rivalries. There have been times when the two clubs have genuinely detested each other, especially in the early days when Woolwich Arsenal were seen as encroaching on Tottenham's patch after they moved from south east London to Highbury in 1913. Matters deteriorated further when football resumed after the War in 1919. Spurs had finished bottom in the last season before hostilities but expected to be reprieved from relegation when the First Division was expanded to 22 clubs, with the top two from the second tier gaining promotion and making up the numbers. However, backstreet politics prevailed. Spurs were relegated and Arsenal, who had finished only in sixth place in the Second Division, were promoted in their place. The controversy is still brought up by Spurs fans, the bad feeling exacerbated by the fact that Arsenal have never been out of the top flight since.

Arsenal's arrival in north London was driven by its chairman, Sir Henry Norris, whose disposition to uproot the club from its south London home and relocate it to a growing suburb beside a station on the new underground network, arguing that there were more than enough fans to go round, can be seen as an early indication of football's willingness to sweep tradition aside when commercial advantage beckons.

Herbert Chapman's[8] Arsenal would go on to be the dominant team in English football in the 1930s, winning three successive titles, while Tottenham languished in the second division for most of the decade. Yet they cultivated support by developing one of the finest stadiums of its time, prompting

---

[8] Chapman, a forward, played two seasons for Spurs, 1905-07, scoring 14 goals in 39 Southern League games.

Charles Buchan,[9] an England international and a prolific goalscorer for both Sunderland and Arsenal, who after retirement became a leading journalist, to observe in 1938, 'The Spurs have the most loyal and critical supporters in England. Why? They were the first club in London to place a cover over the shilling man, and the first to devote three sides of the ground to the shilling man. The Spurs can find room for 60,000 people who pay one shilling. No other club can do that.' A far cry from today's similar capacity, where season ticket prices well in excess of £1,000 are not uncommon.

Memories of the early to mid-20th century often reference the fact that it was not unusual for the committed to go and watch Arsenal one week and Spurs the next. But it would be wrong to conclude that there was no friction between the two sets of fans. In Martin Cloake and Alan Fisher's *A People's History of Tottenham Hotspur Football Club*, supporters who remember the era reveal that the nature of rivalry is often in the eye of the beholder. Peter Jack, for instance, didn't recall any problems when the two

---

[9] As well as being a leading journalist of his time, Charles Buchan co-founded the Football Writers' Association and launched *Charles Buchan's Football Monthly* that, as he said, '...has caught on so well (at its peak, the magazine had a circulation of over 250,000), it was obvious that something of the kind was desperately needed.'

teams shared White Hart Lane during the War (Highbury having been requisitioned by the military), saying, 'People weren't quite as ardent about their teams.' On the other hand, Harry Slater remembers that Spurs fans resented Arsenal using White Hart Lane, commenting, 'They've got the worst clutch of supporters… If a player is having a bad game, what's the point of shouting and harassing the bloke? They should be trying to encourage him.'

In 1944, Joe Hulme, a key member of Chapman's imperious Arsenal side, was employed as Spurs' manager. There's no record of the appointment prompting the consternation that the arrival of former Arsenal luminaries Terry Neill or George Graham caused years later; and Hulme earned plaudits for laying the foundations that Arthur Rowe would build upon to such thrilling effect. It was Rowe's team who would be seen as harbingers of a new age, embracing a style that pushed the traditional English approach – exemplified by Arsenal – to one side when they became Second and First Division champions in successive seasons in 1950 and 1951.

It's perhaps here that the roots of a divergence in identity can be most clearly detected. Arsenal had succeeded by exploiting the change to the offside rule in 1925 that required only two, not three, defenders to be goalside of the opposition forward. This change meant it was no longer possible to keep one of the full-backs in the traditional 2-3-5 formation as cover while the other stepped up to catch the opponents offside. Many teams struggled to cope with the extra space the attackers now had. To counter this, Chapman introduced the W-M formation in which a centre-half was moved into a more defensive role in a three-person backline. Some – most notably esteemed football writer Willy Meisl – saw the WM system as defensive smothering, nullifying the attacking ambition that the change in the law sought to promote. He feared it might be the 'death of football'. It wasn't, of course. Arsenal were revered as they went on to claim the championship five times in the 1930s and indeed supplied seven of the England team who defeated recently-crowned world champions Italy in 1934 in a bruising encounter known as the 'Battle of Highbury'.

However, it was Tottenham's Arthur Rowe whose push-and-run style was eventually seen as the more progressive and exciting application of new ideas. Rowe quietly revolutionised the English game but didn't get the recognition he deserved, perhaps because of his modesty and unassuming manner. All the same, he set the stage for Bill Nicholson's team to attain the first modern Double in 1961 (defeating Arsenal home and away in the process) and then become the first British side to win a European trophy, the Cup Winners Cup in 1963. 'The Spurs Way' was established: entertaining, attack-minded football played by a team liberally sprinkled with stardust. Irving Scholar, the former Tottenham Chairman, remembers them as 'players who would still make a best-ever Spurs team from all sides since the War. I've always believed that a really successful team contains at least three world-class players. And Spurs, at that time, had probably four in White, Mackay, Blanchflower and Jones. Four of the best players ever to play for Tottenham. Each one of those four could walk into any team at any time.'

Spurs were now the masters in their own and their neighbours' backyards. They were the right team in the right place at the right time, and with the success came glamour and fame. As Danny Blanchflower memorably expounded in his famous quote, 'Football is not really about winning or goals or saves or supporters… it's about glory. It's about doing things in style, doing them with a flourish; it's about going out to beat the other lot, not waiting for them to die of boredom; it's about dreaming of the glory that the Double brought.' And so, even when Arsenal replicated Spurs' Double accomplishment ten years later, it seemed somehow diminished by comparison. No matter that the League was, infuriatingly for Spurs, captured on a tumultuous night at White Hart Lane; Spurs had done it first and with more panache – they were the Team of the Century.

By the 1970s, the rivalry had developed a violent edge off the pitch, reflecting the growing hooliganism of the times. A fan was unlikely to go and see both sides regularly, with concepts of loyalty being more defined and less forgiving. The perception of Spurs as entertainers and Arsenal as dull destroyers began to take on a momentum of its own, with each set of fans increasingly rallying around their own standard. Even when George Graham's Arsenal began to establish clear water between themselves and an increasingly directionless Spurs in the 1990s, Spurs fans were happy to mock 'Boring, boring Arsenal' while Arsenal fans chorused their love of the 'one nil to the Arsenal' scoreline.

Over the years, a number of sliding doors moments have added to the complexity of the rivalry. In one, France international Emmanuel Petit went to talk to Spurs, then borrowed a taxi fare to go down the road to sign for the other lot. He went on to become a key member of Arsenal's 1998 Double-winning side. Fans were incensed, but Spurs owner Alan Sugar took it in good part – something that Arsenal Vice Chairman David Dein acknowledged as relations between the boardrooms thawed. Sugar's son's friendship with Dein's daughter probably helped, too.

But what if Petit had chosen Spurs? And what if Spurs had chosen Dutch playmaker Denis Bergkamp who, in another sliding taxi doors moment, repeatedly urged his agent to contact Spurs about signing him even as he was driven to Highbury. Bergkamp had been an admirer of Glenn Hoddle and Tottenham, but Sugar and his manager Gerry Francis turned down the chance to sign someone they viewed as an expensive luxury. Bergkamp went on to be arguably the single most influential factor in Arsenal's transformation. Along with Manchester United, they dominated the early years of the Premier League. Tottenham's decision-making appeared parsimonious and lacking in ambition by comparison.

Perhaps most intriguingly of all, Arsène Wenger could have become Tottenham Hotspur's manager.

In the 1980s, there was a close relationship between Spurs and Monaco. During the French League winter break, Monaco were regular visitors to north London with an Anglo/French friendly trophy at stake. The agent, Dennis Roach,[10] was both a conduit to and a confidant of the two clubs and when the fixture ceased, he used to arrange for Monaco manager Wenger to get his fix of the English football he adored. First stop was usually White Hart Lane before moving on to Highbury and Anfield.

On one of these trips, Alex Fynn, who was advising Spurs on media at the time, fell into

---

[10] Roach also acted as the matchmaker in the subsequent love affair between a former Spurs hero and a future Arsenal one when he brokered the deal that took Glenn Hoddle to Monaco where Wenger built his team around him. 'He is indispensable,' said Wenger. 'We know that. He allows his colleagues to express themselves. All teams need this.'

conversation with Wenger in the Tottenham board room. When Wenger waxed lyrical about his trip and English football, Fynn asked him if he could ever see himself working in England. If so, he continued, 'this is your natural home'. Wenger's attacking style was perfectly aligned to the Tottenham tradition which, sadly, had been pushed to one side at the time.

But it was not to be. Keith Burkinshaw had resigned as Spurs manager to be replaced by his assistant Peter Shreeves,[11] whose inexperience allowed Scholar to take a more hands-on approach to playing matters while he pondered who might be a more weighty successor. He had one name in mind – Terry Venables, who at that time was in charge at Barcelona. Ironically, it would be the man they called El Tel who, along with Alan Sugar, eventually ousted Scholar when the club looked like it might be forced

---

[11] Aware that Burkinshaw was unhappy about the turn of events and had left the club with the withering observation 'There used to be a football club over there', Peter Shreeves was wary of the influence Alex Fynn might have. So when, in a meeting to keep the manager informed of the advertising plans, Fynn suggested that, from a marketing point of view, signing Mario Kempes – arguably the standout star of Argentina 1978 World Cup winners and who was on trial at White Hart Lane – would be a good move, Shreeves defensively replied, 'You must allow me to pick the team.'

into administration. Tottenham Hotspur plc, the first football club to go public, had moved too far and too fast for the times, diversifying into non-football areas with the laudable objective of providing additional funds for the football club only for the businesses to fail and land the whole enterprise with a mountain of debt.

Spurs' loss was Arsenal's gain as David Dein, by serendipity, met up with Wenger at Highbury. It was *coup de foudre* (love at first sight), destiny for Dein who saw Arsène for Arsenal written in the stars. The duo proceeded to launch Arsenal on an unparalleled run of success culminating in the Invincibles season of 2005.

If circumstances had allowed, though, Spurs could have hired a manager even more ultimately successful than Wenger. After breaking the 'old firm' duopoly for the first time in 15 years and becoming Scottish Champions in 1980, Aberdeen continued onwards and upwards. In 1983, they overcame Real Madrid to win the European Cup Winners Cup, then SV Hamburg to win the European Super Cup, and the following season collected a League and Cup double. Their manager, Alex Ferguson, was obviously destined for bigger and better tests of his growing reputation.

After Jock Stein's untimely death in the World Cup playoff game against Wales that took Scotland to Mexico, Ferguson took over as the national manager but failed to get the team out of the group stage, and he stepped down from the role in June 1986.

Scholar sensed a marvellous opportunity to upgrade from the trophy-winning Burkinshaw and with speed, stealth, and secrecy, as Spurs were not the only club casting envious eyes on Ferguson, eventually a Paris rendezvous was arranged. The two men got on well enough and after phone calls back and forth, with Scholar asking, 'Are we ready yet?', a second meeting was held in Paris. Scholar brought along his co-owner, Paul Bobroff, and the three men shook hands on the deal, with all aspects of the contract agreed, for Ferguson to become the manager of Tottenham Hotspur Football Club. Their fellow directors, to a man, were enthusiastic endorsers of the choice but one of them was indiscreet, so the news spread like wildfire within the inner circle only to be dashed almost immediately. Unfortunately, Mrs Ferguson was not keen on a move to London and that was that.

(In November 1986, Ron Atkinson was fired as Manchester United's manager and replaced by Ferguson.)

When Scholar mentioned to his friend, Martin Edwards, the Chairman of Manchester United, that his manager could have been a Spurs man, Edwards refused to believe him. When, out of curiosity, he tackled Ferguson about the story, Ferguson averted his gaze and didn't reply. Edwards subsequently told

Scholar, 'Now I believe you and know you were telling the truth.'

*

Spurs endured a period in the doldrums as a plethora of managers came and went. One of the toughest things for their fans to accept, as Arsenal disappeared over the horizon, was that the kind of stylish football traditionally played in N17 was being offered down the road, while Tottenham were seemingly not only waiting for the opposition to die of boredom, but happy to inflict the same emotion on their own fans.

These days, the divide is pretty clearly defined, and it is an atypical person who would admit to split loyalties. One of the most divisive episodes attracting opprobrium and admiration in unequal measure, according to where loyalty resided, was prompted by Sol Campbell's move across the great divide in 2001.[12] The deed had been done before without

---

[12] The only Spur with a similar standing to move from White Hart Lane to Highbury was Pat Jennings. Deemed erroneously superfluous after 596 appearances, the Northern Ireland international proceeded to keep goal for Arsenal 327 times. Welcomed back to Spurs as a player, coach and ambassador, Jennings is rightly regarded as a true Tottenham hero and with great affection by all who know him.

causing any strife, but it was the manner and timing of the manoeuvre, and its effects, that unleashed a torrent of ill feeling. Campbell had come up through the Spurs youth system, was the club captain, and was seen as the basis upon which a team could be built to take them out of the mediocrity that seemingly had enveloped them. Further, his decision to move after running down his contract was a heavy financial blow and the impression that he thought he was more likely to win things with Arsenal was always going to rankle.

By his past public pronouncements, Campbell had made a rod for his own back. In December 2000, he said, 'Being a Spurs fan as a boy and a player for so many years, it would be hard to sign for Arsenal. I don't think the fans here would ever forgive me.' Under any circumstances, the move – he subsequently signed for Arsenal in July 2001 – would never have gone down well, but the manner of it left Spurs fans feeling they and their club had been strung along. None of which excuses the vitriol still flung his way even after all these years. In 2022, recalling when Campbell was a guest on his programme *My Sporting Life* on *Talksport*, four years earlier, Spurs fan Danny Kelly felt, 'He (Campbell) has regrets about it. There is a part of him that really regrets what happened and the fact that he can't lose it now, that people won't forgive him.'

But while the rivalry crosses the line sometimes, on other occasions, the good in people can shine through. Before the fixture at Highbury in 2018, there was apprehension in some quarters that Spurs fans would not respect the minute's silence for Arsenal hero David Rocastle, who had tragically died of cancer aged just 33. In the event, it was impeccably observed. More recently, after Arsenal star Bukayo Saka was racially abused by bigots and idiots on social media after missing a penalty for England in the European Championship final, Spurs fans displayed a banner proclaiming, 'North London stands with Bukayo Saka and all players against racism and discrimination' at the first derby following the final.

*

With seven games played in the 2022/2023 season, Arsenal proudly led the Premier League, with Spurs one point adrift. Thus, considerably more than parochial plaudits were at stake in this rare top-of-the-table clash. The game kicked off at 12.30pm, a time favoured by the police as it doesn't allow too long in the pubs beforehand, and by the broadcasters as a regular slot with appeal across worldwide time zones (the match was viewed in more than 150 countries). The Emirates was packed, and noisy, challenging the notion of Arsenal's home ground being as quiet as a library, until the back and forth of fan chants was drowned out by some dubious musical concoction, blaring out as the teams took the field.

Conte stuck to his guns with no extra man in midfield to guard against being overrun. When the game kicked off, Spurs, as is so often the case, seemed overawed by the occasion. No matter that the team contained experienced personnel honed in fiercely contested derbies across various cultures and continents; a trip across town to Stamford Bridge or the Emirates invariably saw them withdraw into their shell. Spurs hadn't triumphed at the old enemy's ground in 11 consecutive league attempts, since a 3-2 win in November 2010.

It was one-way traffic for the opening period, culminating in Thomas Partey's stupendous strike to put the hosts one up. Spurs had been sitting off and allowing the opposition to come to them in front of a deep defensive line. The tactic works pretty well as long as an opponent doesn't exploit the space to pull off something spectacular. Partey did. One nil to the Arsenal injected even more energy into the hosts whose guile and power made Spurs look insipid.

Then, against the run of play, Kane equalised from the penalty spot 11 minutes later (his 100th away goal in the top flight) and half time was reached with the score even. It was still, just, possible to believe Conte's plan could work. Although Spurs had clearly been second-best, they were still in the game. But shortly after the restart, Hugo Lloris spilled a shot from Saka, the usually reliable Romero failed to deal with it, and Gabriel Jesus pounced to make a Spurs resurrection unlikely. They folded with half an hour to play after the erratic Royal was sent off for a foolish, needless challenge on Gabriel Martinelli, and when Granit Xhaka added a third shortly after, there was no coming back.

Conte's system demands precision and accuracy and, as he pointed out in his post-match analysis, there might have been a very different outcome if the last crucial passes had not gone astray so often. All the same, if you let a good side – as Arsenal brimming with confidence undoubtedly were – come on to you, then you are inviting disaster. The problem is magnified by a lack of creativity when Kulusevski is absent, as there is no natural playmaker in the side.

Moreover, it was bizarre for Conte seemingly to accept defeat. It is justifiable to bring on defenders (Richarlison and Son were replaced by Sessegnon and Doherty) to protect a 2-0 lead but not when facing a 3-1 deficit. It was as if Conte was thinking, 'I have never shipped six goals and I'm not about to start now.' The substitutions were embarrassing as they flew in the face of how Spurs fans wanted to see their team perform. They certainly didn't want to see their manager appear to throw in the towel. One fan suggested, 'He's thinking about Frankfurt on Tuesday' (the next Champions League fixture). It's a truism that pragmatism is a prerequisite when managing any squad through a season, but sometimes you have to play the match you are in to the bitter end, rather than prioritise the next one. Especially if it's against Arsenal.

Away fans unfortunate enough to be in the proximity of the segregation space had insult literally added to injury. As one recalled, throughout the entire game, and with increasing gusto as events took a turn for the worse, three individuals in particular kept up a constant barrage of vitriol and taunting. It is pathetic that abuse is touted as a natural part of football at all levels today, but these characters took it to new depths.

It's not, it should be pointed out, a phenomenon exclusive to Arsenal. Pretty much every club has an unpleasant minority who seem to think support consists of being as vile as possible and spending the entire match without apparently even glancing at the pitch, such is the dedication to 'bantering' the opposition fans. It's an odd way to spend a lot of money, and it makes for a thoroughly unpleasant afternoon for those on the receiving end. Four times, a father with his eight-year-old son, who was right on the segregation line and subject to a torrent of insults, asked the police to intervene. Four times they didn't. When the second goal went in, one Spurs fan felt a cup of liquid thrown from the top tier hit the back of his jacket. He turned to the policeman beside him and said, calmly, 'They are throwing stuff onto us from the top tier.' And the policeman's response? 'You're all as bad as each other.' It beggars belief.

For Spurs fans, the best way to deal with the disaster of the day was to get away after the final whistle and do something that had little to do with football. However, many found it hard to put their disappointment to one side. Discussion flourished about Conte's strategy – nothing that came anywhere near suggesting he was the wrong man for the job, simply attempts at a measured assessment. He seemed determined to stick with his 3-4-3, whatever the challenge. Formations are, it has to be pointed out, far more fluid during a game than many acknowledge, so a 3-4-3 can be a 5-3-2, 5-2-1-2, 3-4-1-2, or even a 3-5-2 depending on the phase of play, but Conte's selection and tactics seemed to often leave his side one short in the middle.

The team also lacked guile; they played percentage football, hoping to capitalise on mistakes rather than creating chances. Kane would often drop back as a temporary playmaker, at the expense of his presence up front where he was most needed. Kulusevski's absence through injury deprived the team of a viable alternative, his willingness to take defenders on and attack key areas on the edge of the box complementing rather than replicating the threat posed by the other strikers. But hadn't Conte pressed for a squad to deal precisely with this situation, to provide options and strength in depth? Yves Bissouma, bought as the potential answer for more creativity in the middle, had barely featured. Royal didn't do the job a Conte wing-back needed to do, but neither Matt Doherty – a natural wing back – or Djed Spence – who Conte had pointedly described as a club signing – had got a decent look in.

The criticism following the game irritated Conte, prompting an outburst about 'teaching football to many people'. All of us who watch the game have an element of the armchair manager about us, but the truth is that we don't see the players day-to-day; we don't pick up the fine details about mentality and ability that a professional coach must take into account. It is, however, a bit curmudgeonly to hold down such a high-profile job and expect never to be questioned.

At the end of the previous season, Spurs had demolished Arsenal, but despite their current league position, they looked a pale shadow of that team. Moreover, if the substitutions were aimed at preserving players for the Champions League tie three days later, why leave Kane on the pitch? He was the slowest striker in a lone role, and yet more minutes were accruing for the talisman who had played so many games over the last few years, and who would surely be vital in Germany.

As Arsenal basked in the confidence of confirming their place as the number one team of the moment, the question that started to be asked again and again was could they sustain their challenge? In turn, doubts were beginning to creep in about whether the top sides had worked Tottenham out. Just as against

Chelsea, where they were fortunate to come away with a point, Spurs had struggled against a high-intensity opponent who brushed aside all attempts to frustrate them. What if? A different outcome and Arsenal could have been exposed as pretenders and Spurs cemented as real challengers. That, along with all the local pride and one-upmanship, is what makes this derby so special.

Don't let anyone tell you it doesn't matter.

6. ISTANBUL OR BUST

To leave your old rivals firmly ensconced at the top of the Premier League table after coming off a poor second-best in the North London derby was not ideal preparation for a hectic schedule that would see Spurs having to play eight more games before the 1st of November, four of which were crucial and would decide whether or not they qualified for the knockout stages of the Champions League. It would prove to be a tumultuous time.

Three days after the debacle at The Emirates, Spurs were in Germany to face Eintracht Frankfurt in the third tie of the UEFA Champions League group stage. Their opponents represented a shining light in these more cynical times due to a house style that was ambitious, easy on the eye, and successful, having risen from Bundesliga relegation candidates in 2016 to the Europa League Champions in 2022.[13]

In the 1990s, the club was given the nickname *Launische Diva* (Moody Diva) after acquiring a trait of overcoming renowned opposition whilst succumbing to those they were expected to defeat; circumstances

---

[13] Eintracht Frankfurt will always be associated with the European Cup final of 1960, which saw them demolished by an imperious Real Madrid of Di Stefano, Puskas, Gento, *et al* at Glasgow's Hampden Park.

with which Spurs fans could readily identify. As with many Bundesliga clubs, over the course of a season, Frankfurt filled more than 90% of its stadium capacity with an average attendance of 47,000 fervent fans. However, on this night, all present – including around 3,000 travelling devotees – had to summon every ounce of passion to get involved in a turgid encounter.

To be fair, Tottenham showed some improvement on the weekend's dire display, but as the contest petered out in a 0-0 draw, *The Guardian*'s Jonathan Liew observed, 'The sense of treading water is unmistakable'. He went on to pose questions that echoed the concerns of many Spurs fans. 'What's the point of all this? Where is this team going? Does it all just click at some stage? Or does it atrophy and drift, a club whose sole aim of existence is to keep the same players together so they can do this all again next year?'

Antonio Conte had pre-empted any criticism that his style of play might lead to a draw. 'Otherwise (if attack is prioritised) it can happen. You can concede six, seven or eight goals', he said in his pre-match press conference. 'In England, that happens a lot of times. In my career, it never, never happened. I don't like to play open and concede a lot of space. I won in England and then I won in my past and I think I can teach football to many people'. However, it looked like it was going to take longer than he thought to get a wholehearted commitment to his philosophy.

During Arsenal's 19 consecutive seasons in the Champions League, Spurs fans had mocked them for seemingly being content just to qualify and often falling at the first hurdle. 'What's the point unless you try to win it?' they queried. Were Spurs now in danger of emulating their neighbours? As with Arsenal, would those in charge be more bothered about where the money was?

Then – out of the blue – tragic news put all matters into perspective. On the 6th of October, the club's fitness coach, and Conte's long-time friend and colleague, Gian Piero Ventrone, died of a brain haemorrhage. A few days earlier he had learned he had acute myeloid leukaemia. Ventrone had been nicknamed *the marine* because of his rigorous training schedules, but despite this, he was adored by the players. In a relatively short time, he had become a most respected and popular figure, his effect on the team's wellbeing clearly evident; his character and humanity were appreciated by all who worked with him. He had been closely associated with Conte since they were first together at Bari in 2007, and the manager was clearly devastated, with tears visible on several occasions.

The press conference scheduled to run ahead of the weekend game at Brighton was cancelled, but life and the demands of the Premier League roll on regardless. On this particular Saturday evening in Sussex, everyone involved with Tottenham Hotspur Football Club had to try and get down to business as usual. The away end at the Amex Stadium was festooned with Italian flags, and fans chanted, 'There's only one Gian Piero'.

A tight game, in which the home side caught the eye more than the visitors, nevertheless ended in Spurs' favour courtesy of a solitary goal by Harry Kane. Brighton's early-season momentum was stalled, and the visitors had dug out three valuable points to stay in the top three. At the final whistle, captain Hugo Lloris displayed a shirt bearing Ventrone's name in front of the away section as players and fans paid their respects.

*

Four days later, Frankfurt came to North London as the tussle for precious Champions League points resumed. In the vast expanse of the single-tier South Stand, the THFC Flags grassroots fan group had opted to fly just one banner, bearing the face of Ventrone, as a further mark of respect after his untimely passing. A minute's applause before kick-off also acknowledged John Duncan, who had worn the Lilywhite shirt with distinction between 1975 and 1979, and had died at the age of 73.[14] The power of

---

[14] A Scottish striker whose league goals – 53 in 103 appearances – were vital and whose absence through injury was a key factor in the team's relegation in 1977. His return played an important part in Spurs' promotion to the First Division the following season.

so many people joining in common purpose for a brief moment of tribute always impresses.

The match itself proved to be one of the most engaging of the season so far, evoking the tradition of those glory, glory nights whilst giving Conte first-hand experience of what it was really like to hitch your wagon to the topsy turvy fortunes of Tottenham Hotspur.

A crowd of 55,180 in the stadium was significantly enough under capacity to raise questions about the pricing policy once again for the three group-stage home games. The official line was that 'security concerns' had prevented a full house, but empty seats were clearly visible in the most expensive sections of the East and West Stands. Maybe the presence of a particularly affluent hooligan tendency had been anticipated. In fact, the Eintracht fans turned out to be the best and least troublesome of visitors; a contrast to the Marseille ultras, who had caused such problems in the previous home tie. Throughout the game, they kept up a barrage of noise and coordinated scarf twirling that provided quite a spectacle, and they played their part in making the evening one to remember.

But it was the action on the pitch that really drew the eye, especially a stellar performance from Son Heung-Min. The line-up featured three changes from Saturday, with Emerson Royal – his suspension not applicable in Europe – Clément Lenglet, and

Richarlison replacing Doherty, Ben Davies, and Yves Bissouma. When Daichi Kamada put the visitors ahead after 14 minutes after a sloppy pass from, of all people, Cristian Romero, the lingering doubts about Conte's record in this competition looked set for another airing. Those doubts lasted all of seven minutes until Kane set up Son for an equaliser. It was the 50th time the duo had collaborated for a goal. The old one-two was back in business, with Son – in particular – mesmerising the opposition defence and Richarlison's tireless running helping to create space for the pair to exploit.

Eight minutes after the equaliser, Kane was bundled over in the box and – after VAR corrected the referee's initial assessment that no foul had been committed – his penalty put Spurs ahead and cranked up the volume from the stands. Entertainment and passion – whatever next?

Frankfurt weren't giving up though, and narrowly missed drawing level just minutes later. Then Pierre-Emile Højbjerg crossed and Son despatched a volley of such perfection that it could be viewed a hundred times and still demand one more look. It was the kind of magnificent strike that is greeted with a nanosecond of stunned silence before the roar of sheer elation kicks in. And, just for a minute or so, it stunned even the boisterous visitors into silence. At 3-1, and with half an hour played, Spurs were in control and cruising.

But this was Spurs.

Early in the second half, Ryan Sessegnon twice went close, and Son continued to terrorise the opposition; so much so that Frankfurt's Tuta was forced into committing two infringements on him in the space of five minutes. Son, desperate for his hat-trick, tried to continue even after the whistle had sounded and the red card was shown to Tuta. Play was halted as Tuta trudged off, serenaded by a lusty chorus of *Auf Weidersehn* from the home support. With Frankfurt now down to 10 men and with a two-goal deficit, it was surely just a case of seeing the game out.

But this was Spurs.

There ensued an unnecessarily fraught and frantic last 10 minutes. Spurs dropped their intensity and gifted Faride Alidou a second goal. There was no discernible formation, with Kane, Richarlison, Lucas Moura and Bryan Gil all on the pitch whirling at the opposition. Kane flung over a cross, but Gil, due to his lack of height, couldn't rise to it. Undeterred, Gil then careened into the box and, after foregoing a chance to shoot, was clumsily clouted to the turf. A patent penalty. Up stepped Kane. He rarely misses from the spot.

But this was Spurs.

Kane set himself, executed the familiar run-up and skied the kick; absolutely skied it. Frankfurt took heart and pressed forward once more. The crowd were on tenterhooks and the final whistle was greeted with relief. Spurs had been 3-1 up against 10 men and came close to handing Frankfurt a draw. They now topped the group, and victory against their next opponents, Sporting Lisbon, would see them through to the last 16. Following the game, Antonio Conte reflected, 'We conceded a corner, they scored, then we missed the penalty. When we missed the penalty, I admit I was a bit scared, because I thought everything can happen.' A sentiment that could vie with 'To Dare is to Do' or 'The Game is about Glory' to encapsulate the fact that following Tottenham invariably disturbs your equanimity.

And yet it is nights such as these that make the experience of being a Spurs fan so special. Nights when flaws are apparent, but so are patches of perfection; the Spurs' fans definition of 'Spursy'. This was not one of the great glory nights, Son's volley notwithstanding, that will be referenced when the greatest hits compilations are put together. All the same, this was football as it should be played: inspiring, frustrating, frightening, involving, enraging, and ultimately rewarding. And for those who were present, it will live long in the memory because it epitomised why being there is so important.

*

Before the next European night rolled around, Spurs had to navigate three Premier League fixtures in eight days: home games against Everton and

Newcastle interspersed by a trip to Old Trafford. First up were Everton, whose sole purpose seemed to be to clutter the pitch up for 90 minutes. Goals from Kane – a successful spot kick this time – and Højbjerg secured a 2-0 win in which Spurs never really impressed, but then didn't have to in order to secure three points.

Manchester United away, always one of the focal points of the season, was scheduled for a midweek evening to comply with one of the Premier League's three domestic paymasters, Amazon Prime. Committed armchair fans were now required to buy three subscriptions: Sky, BT (who also broadcast the three UEFA competitions), and Amazon. The Premier League and their broadcast partners are exceptionally good at getting money out of their customers; what rankles is that they say this isn't their primary objective.

Tottenham's performance at Old Trafford was about as far from prime as it was possible to be. Despite knowing that victory would move them up to second place behind Arsenal, Spurs left Manchester in the same abject manner that they had the Emirates, this time with a 2-0 loss after providing their hosts with a much-needed confidence boost. They couldn't pass, they couldn't tackle, they showed little ambition, and only Lloris emerged with any credit for preventing a walloping. It was a wretched night, the more so for supporters who had travelled from the south and faced a difficult journey home with no trains running after the final whistle.

So, that was one point from a possible nine in three away games against Chelsea – a fortuitous draw – Arsenal, and Manchester United. More disturbing was the unfortunate habit of giving the top teams the freedom to attack them. Manchester United fired off 28 shots, the most recorded in the Premier League so far this season, following on from the 22 by Arsenal, and 16 by Chelsea. A conspicuous contrast with the controlled displays against Brighton, Everton, and (the last 10 minutes excepted) Eintracht Frankfurt. It was the 39th time Tottenham had been beaten by Manchester United in the Premier League; their worst record against any opponent.

'Not a good game for us, (and) I have to be honest, this was not the first time for us this season', Conte reflected. 'Despite that, the table is good. Every time we play a high-level game, we struggle. Against Chelsea, they dominated the game. Arsenal we lost, and today we lost. When the level is high, we are going to struggle'. Not a message that Spurs supporters wanted to hear. On the evidence, though, a painful truism.

*

Newcastle United were next, arriving in a rich vein of form that heralded the spectre of a league dominated by two state-backed clubs. Would they, like Chelsea and Manchester City, leave Spurs trailing in their wake? The nagging doubts about what the future might bring increased as Spurs, despite Conte switching to five in the middle to bolster his defence, once again began badly.

Two avoidable errors by Lloris – a precipitous rush out of his area and a misplaced pass – gifted Newcastle a 2-0 half-time lead and a now familiar chorus of boos accompanied the home team as they left the pitch. (A Biblical downpour seemed to indicate even the gods were peeved with what they had witnessed.) Newcastle almost added a third soon after the restart, but then Kane got one back from yet another set piece and the crowd got behind their team, urging them on and directing their irritation at the time-wasting antics of visiting keeper Nick Pope. All to no avail. Newcastle held their nerve and Spurs had dropped six points in a week, not the ideal preparation for a vital Champions League tie. Would they be able to raise themselves for a chance to break the cycle of despair and qualify for the last 16?

*

Whatever the resentment about the cost of tickets, a crowd of just under 60,000 – pretty much capacity once the obligations to UEFA and their sponsors, broadcasters, and television production units had been met – were in place for the Sporting Lisbon game.

'You're paying for the facilities', fans are constantly told. Yet by kick-off in the general admission areas of the multi-million-pound stadium (with, ahem, the thousand pound-plus season tickets), the pies ran out, the sausage rolls ran out, the chocolate bars ran out, and one of the most popular beers ran out.

On the pitch, meanwhile, running out was the sum total of Spurs' contribution to the first half. 'The first 45 minutes were an insult to supporters', wrote Tim Spiers in The *Athletic*. 'This was a sizeably important Champions League clash, a big European night, a massive crowd, a ramped-up pre-match atmosphere and Spurs played like it was an early July pre-season friendly away at Barnet'. Not turning up before half time with dire consequential effects was becoming infuriatingly predictable, and it was therefore no surprise when Marcus Edwards put Sporting ahead, and the awful prospect arose that Spurs might not even progress beyond the group stage.

Although, as usual, the pace was picked up in the second half, it wasn't until the 80th minute that Rodrigo Bentancur headed Spurs level and then went close in stoppage time. Just an appetiser for what was to follow. With the last kick of the game, in the 96th minute, Kane fired home from an Emerson Royal header to spark pandemonium and elation. It was a last-minute winner that meant so much and the noise and celebrations around the ground were palpable. Spurs were through to the round of 16. However, as ecstatic fans began to compose themselves, they noticed players and staff gesticulating, and no one returning to the centre circle to restart the game.

Then, surely not? After a five-minute conflab, by the tightest of margins the goal was ruled out for offside. As Conte went ballistic on the pitch in the middle of a melee of players, staff, and officials, the final whistle must have sounded, but few noticed. Spurs were now faced with the prospect of travelling to Marseille with a draw the minimum requirement for qualification.

After the game, Conte – obsessed with the VAR decision – fulminated, 'I'd like to see if you take this type of decision for a top team in an important game. I'd like to see if the VAR is so brave to take this decision (endorsing the goal) a fair decision because the ball is in front of Kane.

'Sorry, but I'm really upset because sometimes you can accept situations. Sometimes it's not good because I don't see honesty in this situation. When I don't see this, I become really upset… but now, because of this decision, we have to wait for the last game against Marseille. I repeat, this decision creates big damage.

'I hope the club understands this and then, in the right situation, speak with the people we need to speak to. Otherwise, it's only the manager. The club has to be strong.'

VAR has now been around long enough to be thanked and cursed in equal measure. Any watching Manchester City fans could not be blamed for thinking what goes around comes around after being on the receiving end of an equally controversial decision that put Spurs through at their expense to the Champions League semi-final in 2019.

Those present in the stadium were left utterly deflated. There are few pleasures like the exultation of a last-minute winner, especially one that has turned a game on its head. That feeling of elation is one of the game's great delights. But instead of an adrenalin rush, the sort of high that makes sport so compelling, VAR – whichever way the decision falls – undermines the moment. And if vital spontaneous moments are taken away, are the exorbitant ticket prices worth paying?

In this instance, after much examination, poring over still images and slowed-down video, after drawing lines and measuring pixels and delving ever deeper to come up with increasingly complex reasons, the decision to rule out the goal appeared to be the right one. Because it was a last-minute incident, with so much at stake, an inordinate amount of time, more than five minutes, was taken over deliberating. But, surely, if more than two or three minutes are not sufficient to decide if a mistake has been made, then the referee's original decision should stand.

The great justification for VAR was supposed to be that it would eliminate clear and obvious errors. More often than not, it does, but if the regulations require the process to take into account such controversial points as non-deliberate defensive touches, the separation of segments of play lasting seconds into 'phases', and the examination of individual video frames, maybe legitimate human error by the referee is preferable. Of course, that can enrage and frustrate but, right or wrong, it's over – *finito!* – and the here and now of elation and despondency is preserved.

Conte's rage had led to him being red-carded, so he would be unable to communicate with his team before or during the final decisive group game against Marseille. What's more, he'd questioned the integrity of the system, prompting UEFA to say it would investigate. Before the crucial trip to the south of France, however, there was an important fixture on the south coast of England.

*

Against Bournemouth, Conte fielded three defensive midfielders in a 5-3-2/3-5-2 formation and benched Dier and Bentancur who had played 99% and 91%, respectively, of Spurs' 1,530 minutes of the season so far, though he still started with Kane (99%), Højbjerg (93%), and Son (90%). Circumstance seemed to be dictating a pragmatic move away from the 3-4-3 he had appeared to prefer, but formations are only a flexible means to an end, and the lack of any creativity and attacking resources from the continued absence of both Kulusevski and

Richarlison were the primary issues. Forty-nine minutes in, and Spurs trailed 2-0.

At half-time, a further change had seen Lucas Moura introduced for Oliver Skipp to bolster the attack. Just before the hour, Ryan Sessegnon weaved his way into the box to put Spurs back in the game, and Conte rolled the dice. On came Eric Dier to settle the back line in place of Davinson Sánchez, and a minute later Rodrigo Bentancur replaced the somewhat anonymous Yves Bissouma. Spurs laid siege to Bournemouth's goal and turned the screw further when Ivan Perišić replaced Emerson Royal. He proved an inspired choice, crossing for Ben Davies to head Spurs level on 73 minutes.

Spurs now threw everything at their opponents in an attempt to pick them off, securing corner after corner and piling men forward. Two minutes into stoppage time, Bentancur gathered a clearance on the edge of the penalty area and lofted it into the top of the net. Forgetting for the moment the threat of VAR, the away support erupted. There was still room, it seemed, for the outpouring of elation at the prospect of a last-gasp winner. Spurs fan and writer Adam Powley tweeted, '2-0 down 3-2 up, you say? Regardless of opposition and performance, it's the perfect football result. The golden ratio. Michelangelo's *David*. Luther's *Never Too Much*. Nothing comes close.'

When the celebrations were completed, enhanced by the news that further along the coast, Brighton had beaten Chelsea, some of the most dedicated Spurs fans returned home to pack for the airport and fly to the south of France.

*

Following disturbances in north London, concerns had arisen regarding the return fixture. Marseille, even at the best of times, is always a hostile venue – whoever their opponents may be – and the omens for the travelling fans were not good as the northern tribune of the ground (where the local ultras usually gathered) was closed as a result of violence in and around the stadium when Eintracht Frankfurt showed up.

Much preparation goes into these games, necessitating the away club personnel to pay on-site visits to try to eliminate possible problems, especially with how their fans are to be handled. Where fan groups are organised, as at Spurs, they also work with the club, often enlisting the help of Football Supporters Europe (FSE). FSE is always faced with a difficult task, endeavouring to secure understanding and expectation across multiple cultures with different authorities. Belatedly, the organisation managed to get a foot in the door with UEFA, which now recognises it as a legitimate voice of fans. Taking on board what that voice says, rather than just assuming it ticks the consultation box, varies from match to match and from country to country.

The previous season, FSE had worked in conjunction with the Tottenham Hotspur Supporters' Trust and the club in an ultimately unsuccessful challenge to a judicial order from the local municipality in Rennes for the Europa Conference fixture, banning anyone who could be identified as a Spurs fan from specified areas in town for a set period around the game. A further illustration of the French authorities' hard-line approach – their attitude towards all football supporters is to view them as a nuisance or a threat – came with the news that a similar ban was on the cards in Marseille.

The usual to and fro over what restrictions were really necessary resulted in the issuing of a list of what not to do and where not to go. Phone chargers and bags bigger than the size of a small parcel were not allowed, and visiting fans were required to congregate at a given point to wait for buses to ferry them to the ground. They were told to be at the pickup point hours before kick-off, and though it was not possible to say when the last bus went before the match, they were strongly advised not to travel independently in their own interests. The question of whether a game should be convened under such conditions in a place where the authorities admitted they could not fulfil basic safety standards should have been uppermost in the thoughts of UEFA. But, of course, it wasn't.

Some fans cancelled their trips, preferring to take the financial loss rather than the hassle. Many had not applied in the first place. Under the club's ticketing point system, away European ties usually required upwards of 250 points, earned by match attendance. For this one, only 75 were necessary for a ticket, such was the lack of demand. Around 1,000 made the trip. It was possible to stay clear of problems and most did, but the malevolent backdrop was ever-present. And, of course, those that made it to the ground were compelled – from the highest point above the pitch – to watch through fencing grills. For this, Marseille had charged a high price, but then so had Spurs.

On the night, despite the closure of one end of the ground, there were still over 50,000 present and a hostile and confrontational atmosphere prevailed. The evening before, fireworks outside the Spurs hotel had disturbed a good night's sleep, and a corridor of flares subsequently greeted their coach as it arrived at the ground. A supreme test of Spurs' character awaited them. In all their great European history, they had never beaten a French side on French soil and had endured some torrid nights; a prickly encounter in Lyon way back in 1967 in which blows were exchanged and Alan Mullery sent off still comes to mind to supporters of a certain age.

After his red card against Sporting, Conte was forced to watch from a position in the Directors' box just behind Daniel Levy, with his assistant Cristian Stellini in the dugout. Spurs struggled to get going once more; they had trailed at half time in their last three games. All the usual deficiencies were apparent: a lack of creativity in the midfield, little pressing of note, and a complete inability to pose any real threat to the opposition goal.

Events soon went from bad to worse.

Son, dazed after receiving a heavy, albeit accidental, blow across the face was replaced by Bissouma. And the formation was switched to 3-5-2, which at times regressed to 5-3-2, inviting the inevitable assault. Chancel Mbemba's headed goal duly gave Marseille the lead at the break, putting them in line for the Champions League last 16 and demoting Spurs to a place in the Europa League.

Fortunately, the second half also followed the pattern of Spurs' recent encounters. From somewhere, they dug deep, showed stamina, and exhibited their technical ability. They took the game to Marseille, pressed them high up the pitch and were duly rewarded when Lenglet headed in a Perišić free kick. They were now in the runners-up position in the group.

But this was Spurs.

After Højbjerg hit the bar when he should have scored, Said Kolasinac, one of four opponents with an Arsenal pedigree, fortunately headed wastefully wide. Then, in the last minute of stoppage time, rather than take the ball to the corner, Harry Kane put Højbjerg in the clear 20 yards out. Højbjerg steadied himself and shot, sending the ball in off the far post. Spurs now leapfrogged Eintracht Frankfurt, their 2-1 last-gasp triumph putting them into the knockout phase as group winners with 11 points.[15]

'It was a flagrant miscommunication', observed Armine Harit, the Marseille midfielder. His colleague, Matteo Guendouzi, explained, 'If we knew that Frankfurt were winning we wouldn't have gone overboard. We would, at least, have kept our defensive shape.'

Without sounding convincing, Igor Tudor, the Marseille manager, blamed the 'noise' in the stadium. 'It was not possible to explain to the boys (that the draw qualified them for the Europa League). They wanted to score.' And in so doing, they left themselves open to be exposed by Kane and

––––––––––––––––––––

[15] If the goal against Sporting had been awarded, then Spurs, in all probability, would have rested many of the first team for the academic encounter against Marseille. They may well have come away empty handed and finished with 10 points. The necessity to win the last game in the final analysis earned them a retrospective €930,000 for the draw against Sporting.

Højbjerg, who ended their European ambitions for the season.

Before the game, the front-page headline of the local regional newspaper proclaimed 'The match of the year'. Following the defeat, the headline read 'The fiasco of the year'. And in a candid, and to English ears atypical, post-match conference, Tudor admitted he made a mistake. 'I should have given (Demitri) Payet (who was an unused substitute) at least 15 minutes'. In a further frank observation, Tudor said, 'Managers make mistakes every weekend'. For some reason, France international Payet – who had been one of the main reasons for Marseille's Champions League qualification under their previous manager, Jorge Sampaoli – had not been a regular starter all season. His absence was Tottenham's gain as, despite his short stay and manner of leaving, many West Ham fans would acknowledge his skill as a playmaker.

If Bournemouth had been the late show, this was the late, late show. The players and the fans, knowing the job was done, celebrated wildly. In the stands, Conte went berserk, fist-pumping and hugging those around him. Daniel Levy, sitting a row in front, can have been in no doubt what this result meant to his manager or his assistant, Cristian Stellini, who admitted, 'It was very difficult in the first half. But we didn't lose our spirit and stayed in the match. We changed many things in the second half. We discussed how to press them and take control of the match and we played a fantastic second half. We weren't happy with a draw. As always, we pushed on to try and win.'

Whatever the doubts, and many remained on this chaotic, discombobulated night – when Spurs had been first, second, third, and fourth in their group during the course of 90 minutes – the undeniable fact was that they were in the knockout stages.[16] And as a seeded team. One of the top 16 teams in Europe. A further minimum of €9.6 million was guaranteed by UEFA, together with the proceeds of at least one more home fixture, which could amount to as much as £5 million.

Højbjerg's winning goal with the last kick of the game struck a poignant note. He is the type of midfield warrior every team needs. Not always fully appreciated by his audience, but a vital cog in the machine, nonetheless. In an interview for the BBC's *Football Focus* programme, broadcast some days previously, he had also provided some much-needed perspective. He spoke openly and frankly about how,

---

[16] Champions League 2022/23 Group D

	Points	Played	Wins	Draws	Losses	Goals For	Goals Against	+ / -
1.Tottenham	11	6	3	2	1	8	6	+2
2. Frankfurt	10	6	3	1	2	7	8	-1
3. Sporting	7	6	2	1	3	8	9	-1
4. Marseille	6	6	2	0	4	8	8	0

at a relatively young age, he'd had to deal with the terminal illness and death of his father. By sharing his experience, he wanted to make it easier for others to deal with theirs in an age when men, especially, still found it hard to confront their emotions, to admit that sometimes life can be brutal. His candour was the testimony of one top footballer's humanity. Players are, for all the fame and fortune, just human beings subject to the same challenges as the rest of us.

7. SO FAR, SO GOOD

The pubs on Tottenham High Road knew the drill. Chalkboard messages on the pavement mocked some abysmal first half displays: 'Big screen Sunday, Liverpool kick off 16:30, Spurs kick off 17:30'. It was bonfire weekend, and while temperatures were still mild, the afternoons were beginning their slow erosion into dark winter evenings and the tension was crackling as the street lighting came on.

Liverpool had not, by the extraordinary standards they had set over the last few years, made the best of starts. They had failed to win away from home all season, and the red machine was beginning to show signs of wear and tear, probably a result of the enormous physical and mental pressure of having fulfilled every possible fixture the previous season. In the end, they only captured the minor baubles – the League and FA Cups – of the four they had hotly contested to the bitter end.

Normally, Spurs fans would have seen the punchline coming a mile off. But this was Conte's Spurs now and, despite the many unresolved issues, the late fightbacks and tenacious foothold on a top-four place reflected his relentless regime; interminable fitness sessions, tough training, and lengthy team meetings. After being outplayed by Chelsea, Arsenal, and Manchester United, here was another chance to show that Spurs could overcome one of the top teams, albeit one in indifferent form.

The home team, though, were not without the scars of battle, and Conte had to pick from a depleted squad that could not call upon the injured Son Heung-Min or Richarlison. On the other hand, Dejan Kulusevski, who had not featured since September, made a welcome return as a substitute.

Once again, though, Spurs didn't rise to the occasion. It wasn't by any means their worst first half performance, but it was still lacklustre. By contrast, the constant interchanging of Liverpool's front three, with Mohammed Salah popping up all over the place, Darwin Núñez piling into the vast expanses of space left behind Emerson Royal, and Roberto Firmino dropping deep to receive and then shred what passed for a white-shirted midfield, put Spurs on the back foot from the off.

After 11 minutes, Salah, a long-time thorn in Spurs' side (who had first tormented them on an April night in 2013 when Basel knocked them out of the Europa League), put the visitors ahead, by-passing a statuesque home defence. Then, five minutes before the interval, came a dreadful error by Eric Dier. Under no pressure whatsoever, he headed straight to Salah, and the Liverpool forward raced clear to clip the ball over Hugo Lloris.

There was no mistaking the torrent of boos that swept down from the stands as the home team left the pitch at half-time. Their ears were presumably still ringing after Conte had his say and Spurs proved the chalkboard prophecies correct as they took the game to their opponents. Ivan Perišić hit the bar, and a penalty shout was turned down (only for a free kick for a similar offence to be given the other way minutes later). The pace intensified when Matt Doherty and Kulusevski replaced Royal and Ryan Sessegnon in the 68th minute. Within two minutes, Kulusevski's dribble and pass set Kane up to score and prompt thoughts of yet another successful fightback. Not this time, though. Spurs threw everything at Liverpool for the remainder of the match but could not convert their chances.

It had been a rousing conclusion to the weekend, but the undeniable fact was that, once again, Spurs had come up short. Moreover, they had given a much-needed shot in the arm to a key rival. And to add insult to injury, the defeat enabled Newcastle to move above them into third place in the table.

*

Midweek brought a League Cup fixture that stirred memories of some epic clashes against Nottingham Forest in the 1990s. The memories were quickly extinguished after a strong Spurs line-up displayed utter indifference to the competition and ended up well beaten 2-0. Extensive roadworks and diversions on the motorway back to London rounded off an instantly forgettable night for hundreds of southern-based supporters.

*

The final weekend before the Premier League took a break for the World Cup saw Leeds welcomed to the Tottenham Hotspur stadium. What a way to bring down the curtain on act one. Three times the visitors took the lead, and three times they were pegged back by Harry Kane, Ben Davies, and Rodrigo Bentancur. And still the drama was not over. Bentancur had been immense and had put Spurs level on 81 minutes. Two minutes later, with the stadium in a state of bedlam, a deep-lying Kane reverse-clipped the ball into the path of Kulusevski, who powered through the Leeds box to the byline before supplying a subtle pass for Bentancur to slot home.

The mix of elation at the slick, incisive football and the delight at the late winner combined to create one of those moments when you are convinced you are watching the greatest sport on earth. An obviously tired team had managed to raise themselves to record their third eleventh-hour victory in the last four matches, continuing the pattern of digging out points – 13 in the Premier League and seven in the Champions League – from losing positions. Another definition of 'Spursy' to consider: 'They score three, so we will score four.'

In the bars and cars and on trains, buses, and walks home, the excited savouring of a truly special afternoon turned to consideration of how far the team had come under Antonio Conte, and how far Tottenham Hotspur could go once the season recommenced in six weeks' time.

After a distinguished career as a player with Juventus and the Italian national team, Conte had begun his coaching career in Serie B with Arezzo, Bari, and Siena, interspersed with a spell at Atalanta. After getting Bari and Siena promoted to Serie A, he moved to Juventus with astonishing effect, winning three successive titles. He subsequently managed the national team, reaching the quarter-final of the European Championship in 2016 before resuming his successful club career at Chelsea. In West London, he secured both the Premier League and the FA Cup before an acrimonious parting of the ways. With his CV now showing him to be one of a select group of managers who had won championships in more than one major football country, he returned to Italy and won another *Scudetto,* this time with Internazionale. Yet, once again, there were disputes and Conte was soon a free agent. After initially turning Tottenham down in the summer of 2021, he changed his mind.

So, it was just over a year since the 53-year-old Conte arrived at Tottenham on the 2nd of November 2021, when Spurs were eighth in the table and in the wake of a chastening 3-0 thrashing at home by

119

Manchester United. Having barely got his feet under the table, he proceeded to lose to Vitesse Arnhem and then NS Mura, the lowest-ranked team in the lowest tier of European cup football. Conte's response was, 'If anyone thinks I am a magician…' He left the sentence hanging, before adding, 'The only magic I can do is to work'. And work he certainly did.

Always intensely focused, Conte swiftly eliminated the lackadaisical culture that had drifted in under Nuno. There was clarity about what he expected from his players and about the way he wanted them to play. He quickly gained their confidence and he and his staff transformed the atmosphere on and off the pitch into something recognisable as an elite sporting enterprise. There were bumps in the road – four defeats in five games at the turn of the year – and the consequential predictable media outbursts prompting thoughts of a possible exit, but both Arsenal and Manchester United were overtaken to finish in fourth spot with a Champions League place; a world away from the embarrassment of celebrating qualification for the Europa Conference League under José Mourinho.

The accomplishment pointed up the issue that both Conte and his employers had to face; to show they were willing and able to build on what had been achieved in the short term and move forward together. This went straight to the heart of an extremely complex relationship, one that is absolutely pivotal to the future of Tottenham Hotspur.

Conte arrived at Spurs with his eyes wide open. He knew how the club operated, with one of the lowest wages-to-turnover ratios in the Premier League (57% 2020/21) and monumental matchday revenue of over £100 million, augmented by extensive extraneous events such as NFL games and top-of-the-bill boxing bouts. On the downside, because of the debt incurred in the construction of the new stadium – £854 million in bank borrowings in 2021– the club was actively seeking some outside financial input.

Spurs have a rich history and all the trappings of a big club, but crucially no contemporary success, something Conte achieved with Juventus, Chelsea and Internazionale. He was not the first top manager Daniel Levy had employed, and an unsuccessful spell would surely prompt searching questions about whether the blame could be laid at the door of the latest incumbent of the managerial hot seat or the two-decade-old regime that had employed him.

Conte was quick to question certain principles and was pleasantly surprised when his request to offload Tanguy Ndombele, Dele Alli, and Giovanni Lo Celso was accepted, despite the financial hit. He seemed to be applying the leverage previous managers had failed to, perhaps rooted in a belief that Spurs needed him more than he needed them. Conte knew the club was aware of his *modus operandi* and, that if he didn't get his way, he could simply refuse to extend his contract.

Conte's preoccupation is not just football but winning football. And he expects everyone to follow his lead and back him to the hilt in his obsession. 'It's very hard, it's very demanding', Cesc Fàbregas, who had played for Arsène Wenger and Pep Guardiola before he arrived at Chelsea, told *The Times*. 'If you want to perform well under him, you need to breathe football, you need to live football 24/7, you need to go to training, ready to spend a lot of energy in areas you probably thought was not possible. You play well for him, you work hard for him, and if you don't and are going your own way, then you will not be in his plans.'

Having turned down Levy's initial offers, Conte was able to negotiate from a position of strength. He insisted on a supporting staff of nine, more than any of his predecessors, and persuaded the club to back him with signings that were made early, another departure from what previous managers had been forced to accept. Over the years, structures and strategies have veered wildly, with the only consistency seeming to be inconsistency as the club switched from one style to another with each new appointment. Successively employing Juande Ramos, Harry Redknapp, André Villas-Boas, Tim Sherwood, Mauricio Pochettino, and José Mourinho does not exactly demonstrate a consistent playing philosophy.

Underlying the changes was the suspicion that the chairman had a tendency to assert his influence to little positive effect.

A case in point; following the implied ground-breaking appointment of Jacques Santini in 2004, the board was left with little alternative but to turn to his assistant, Martin Jol, when Santini walked after just 13 games. Jol probably confounded his employers by stabilising the team and making them a potent attacking force which finished the season in ninth position. In 2005/06, he performed even better, only missing out on Champions League qualification on the last day of the season due to illness which affected many of the players.[17] All the same, fifth place was Spurs' highest league position since 1990. Another fifth place and UEFA Cup qualification was again secured in 2006/07. However, there was the underlying sense that Jol had been Hobson's choice, so it was no great surprise when he was summarily discarded, with the board ostentatiously courting the supposed next managerial big thing, Juande Ramos.

---

[17] Ten players succumbed to food poisoning the night before an off-colour Tottenham lost 2-1 to West Ham, thereby enabling Arsenal to qualify for the last Champions League spot. The mystery illness, which had conspiracy theorists and Arsenal fans rubbing their hands in glee, cost Spurs a place in the top club competition, and the millions of pounds that accompanied it.

He turned out to be yet another let-down but at least won the League Cup with Jol's team.

More recently, Pochettino built the most exciting and successful squad in a generation. Once again, this wasn't quite how the board had envisaged the turn of events. The appointment was believed to have been made primarily in order to steer the team through a difficult stadium build, after which a top, top coach would swoop in to capture the trophies for which Pochettino had painstakingly laid the groundwork. But despite transforming the club from a Europa League one to a Champions League one and contesting the final in 2019, his plea to freshen up his resources fell on deaf ears. And when he failed to assert any leverage he might have possessed, a parting of the ways was on the cards.

It is to Conte's credit that he has firmly asserted that it is he who is indisputably in charge of all football matters, and everything and everybody has to feed his obsession of winning football – although he frequently irritates sections of the support by inferring he is not getting what he wants when it suits him. Despite some woeful first half displays, Conte had got the fans to put aside (for the time being, at least) the old debate about style or success which has dogged the most recent appointees. Starved of trophies for so long, they seemed prepared to prioritise pragmatism over romance and substitute success for entertainment far more than has previously been the case.

Conte's playing strategy of wing-backs and box-to-box midfielders, contrary to the fears of some, has not proved to be sterile. Certainly, at times, it has erred on the side of caution, but it has also raised spirits, particularly with the plethora of eleventh-hour notable displays. In short, as in all his previous appointments, he has improved both the individual and the collective.

A prime example of individual improvement is Ben Davies. The Wales international defender, seen as little more than a workaday squad player by many, has flourished to become a reliable component of the defence, whether operating either as a left-sided centre-back or, his lack of pace notwithstanding, as a more than adequate makeshift wing-back. Under Conte, only Lloris, Højbjerg, Dier and of course Kane have played more than the 4,219 minutes Davies has put in.

Of course, Harry Kane. The beating heart of the team. Only five goals behind Jimmy Greaves's prodigious all-time Tottenham goalscoring record of 266 and within two (with 51 goals in 78 internationals) of Wayne Rooney's England record, Kane left for Qatar and the World Cup as a hero for club and country. A terrific striker, he has shown in the last couple of seasons that he possesses the all-round game to be a top playmaker as well. Not since Glenn Hoddle graced White Hart Lane has anyone witnessed a Spur with the foresight to pick out and the skill to deliver the perfect pass to such effect. As

Kane's number of assists – 23 since 2020 – testify, he is a genuinely innovative team player with a capacity to provide the unexpected. 'One of our own' like Hoddle, Kane is (and Hoddle was) simply irreplaceable.

Kane's Premier League goals so far, 12 in 15 games at a strike rate of 0.81 per 90 minutes, is an exceptional statistic but hasn't received its due acclaim because of the phenomenon that is Erling Haaland. A whirlwind introduction to the Premier League with 18 goals in 13 appearances – 1.56 per 90 minutes – including a hat-trick for City in the Manchester derby for which *L'Equipe* awarded him the rare accolade of 10/10,[18] he has monopolised the headlines.

Not a demonstrative leader, Kane looked positively embarrassed as he resorted to four-letter words during a pre-match exhortation revealed in the Amazon documentary *All or Nothing*. He leads by example, leaving others to do the shouting on the

---

[18] Which brings to mind Ralph L Finn's match report in *The People* on the 15th of October 1960 when, after Tottenham Hotspur's prospective double side thrashed rivals Nottingham Forest 4-0 away from home, he wrote, 'Fabulous, fabulous Spurs. They were perfect, every man Jack of them. And I'm not being pretentious in awarding each of them maximum points (10 out of 10).'

pitch. Surprisingly, wrote Jack Pitt-Brooke in *The Athletic*, 'There are plenty of people out there who do not just underrate Kane, but actively dislike him. He gets plenty of abuse on social media (he is the fifth most abused player on Twitter according to one study) for all sorts of things: the way he tackles, the way he challenges for headers, the way he wins penalties, the way he claims goals, even the way he speaks. It does feel rather excessive when the only controversy Kane has ever been involved in was his brief attempt to engineer a move to Manchester City at the age of 28.' An important member of UEFA would beg to differ. He volunteered the view that, 'I don't like his gamesmanship, the way he wins free kicks and penalties,' but then he is an Arsenal fan.

His admirers, though, outnumber his critics. 'I'm a huge fan of Harry Kane,' Jürgen Klinsmann told *The Athletic* podcast *The View from the Lane*, 'as we all are at Spurs.[19] It's a decision he has to make sooner or

---

[19] Despite playing only 68 games, and scoring 38 goals, in two spells – the second of which saw him become the main contributor in saving Spurs from relegation – Jürgen Klinsmann was regarded with deep affection by all who watched him in the Lilywhite shirt. He loved living in London and playing for Spurs and left only because Franz Beckenbauer, the President of Bayern Munich and formerly his manager when Germany won the World Cup at Italia 90, called him personally and asked him

later (shall I stay or should I go?) He knows he has a very good team right now. He is a very strong-minded man so we all hope he actually starts to win trophies now at Spurs... But I also think people will forgive him if he said at a certain point – if it's next summer or the summer after, when his contract is definitely over – that he will move on to a club that might give him a higher probability to win trophies. But I still have that hope that it will happen with Spurs.'

Klinsmann's hopes may yet be fulfilled this season. The intense schedule of 22 games in 12 weeks had taken its toll with injuries to key personnel – for example, Kulusevski, who missed 13 games, and highlighted the team's lack of creativity. And Son's loss of form, only three goals so far, was of concern too. But still Spurs sat in fourth place in the Premier League and in the last 16 of the Champions League. So far, so good. But questions remained regarding the playing strategy, with some dreadful first half performances and the inability to step up to the mark

_____

to come to the club. Even as a former player for Bayern's arch-rivals Stuttgart, Jürgen felt he could not resist Beckenbauer's appeal. With support from his former teammates, he has also thrown his hat into the ring for both permanent and temporary managerial roles at Spurs. Receiving no encouragement, he has come to the conclusion that: 'The people in charge don't match with me.'

against the top teams fresh in the memory. Not to mention the most important issue of all: Conte's contract. With no commitment beyond the end of the season, neither the club nor the supporters can envisage a long-term plan and what it might entail.

Conte has admitted he has 'an important salary' (£15m per annum),[20] so this was not an issue when he first turned the club down, unconvinced at the time that Spurs shared his ambition for 'winning football' and the commitment it entails. Levy broke the habit of a lifetime to try to accommodate Conte on wages and transfers. Having not obtained all the reinforcements he wanted in the summer (a top right wing-back remains a priority), Conte will undoubtedly push for this position to be fulfilled in January. So, maybe he feels that if he signed a contract extension now, it would weaken his bargaining position. He could legitimately point out to Levy, why build a world-class stadium if you are not prepared to pay the price for world-class players to play there?

---

[20] When Chelsea fired Conte in July 2018 with 12 months left on his contract, it subsequently cost them a payout of £26.6m for him, his staff, and the accompanying legal fees. When they also got rid of Thomas Tuchel in September 2022, it brought their total costs for changing managers since Roman Abramovich took over in 2003, to more than £100m.

Levy is undoubtedly grateful that Conte is his coach and Conte, in turn, says he enjoys being at Spurs. So, the challenge for both of them is to demonstrate, perhaps with a little give and take on both sides, that they are pledged to work together to continue to take the club in the right direction.

8. WORLD IN MOTION

After two years disrupted by Covid-19, there would be no chance for the Premier League in 2022/23 to return to the natural rhythms of a season. Instead, after the tumult of Spurs' 4-3 victory over Leeds United there was… nothing. Or rather a gap, into which a World Cup had been inserted.

As the reality of the tournament in Qatar drew nearer, the anticipation that was usually in evidence as the ultimate footballing competition was about to begin was overshadowed by the controversial choice of the host nation. Of course, the argument that politics should not be mixed with sport was trotted out but awarding the World Cup to Qatar was a political decision in itself, there being little football tradition, culture, or infrastructure to build upon, just promises backed by millions of riyals.

The debate that raged around whether the political system and way of life rendered Qatar an unsuitable venue was criticised as the application of double standards by the West with its plethora of commercial links to the Middle East. In a bizarre speech the day before the tournament opened, FIFA President Gianni Infantino said he empathised with various groups, including migrant workers and gay people, as he himself had suffered prejudice as he was growing up because he had red hair and was an Italian in a Germanic region of Switzerland.

However, the attempts to brush aside legitimate concerns regarding attitudes to women, gay people and the treatment of the thousands of migrant workers without whom the tournament prerequisites – the stadia, hotels, road and rail links – could not have been built, suggested a disturbing attempt to argue against some basic universal human values.

Several countries, including England and Wales, stated their intention to wear a 'One Love' armband to highlight issues of concern. But they were, with brutal clumsiness, threatened with sanctions and backed down, leading to further criticism over lack of genuine commitment even to stick by this watered-down gesture. Unease and outrage were surely not the feelings a competition organiser would hope to spark, but there was plenty of both, along with irritation among supporters, who put club before country, at the break in the season. Boycotting the tournament felt like a futile gesture; watching it wholeheartedly might leave a bad taste in the mouth, but most felt that they would be drawn in at some stage.

A World Cup once provided the opportunity to expand horizons, to discover new talent, but today's game is now a truly global one, and any representative from one of the contenders would undoubtedly be a familiar face to millions. So fans, in addition to the affiliation to their national team, could also look favourably at other countries as they followed the fortunes of players from their clubs. For

Spurs supporters there were 11 representing 10 nations – only Chelsea (12), Manchester United (13) and Manchester City (16) had more. The Spurs contingent was Pierre-Emile Højbjerg (Denmark), Ivan Perišic (Croatia), Richarlison (Brazil), Ben Davies (Wales), Hugo Lloris (France), Eric Dier and Harry Kane (England), Rodrigo Bentancur (Uruguay), Pape Matar Sarr (Senegal), Cristian Romero (Argentina), and Son Heung-Min (South Korea).

After watching Brazil defeat Serbia, Spurs and England fan Doug Bagley, as he travelled back to his hotel on the Metro wearing his Spurs shirt, heard Brazilian fans shouting 'go Spurs' and 'come on Spurs' as they celebrated Richarlison's spectacular strike. Such is the universal appeal of football, and the enhanced reputation and the halo effect on clubs of outstanding feats at the World Cup. But FIFA's largesse means there is even more to be gained.

With 2022 World Cup revenue of $7.5 billion, $1 billion more than in 2018, FIFA could afford to be generous.[21] From the training period a few days

---

[21] With the vast majority of its income earned in a World Cup finals year, it is no surprise that FIFA has expanded its pot of gold. And 48 teams in 2026, up from 32, will grow broadcasting and sponsorship revenue exponentially. However, the search to fill the fallow years in between tournaments has led FIFA to

before the big kick-off until their representatives were eliminated, clubs received $10,000 per day in lieu of their employees' absence, irrespective of whether they actually played. So, the further a country progressed the more money the clubs received. A total of $209 million was shared by 416 clubs. For Spurs, Højbjerg, Davies and Bentancur didn't make it out of their groups. The knockout stage saw Son and Sarr depart at the first time of asking. With six of their men in the quarter-finals – Perišic, Richarlison, Kane, Dier, Romero, and Lloris; three in the semi-final, Perišic, Romero and Loris; and two in the final – Romero and Lloris, Spurs received $2.4 million.

Doug Bagley has an extraordinary dedication to the game, not only following Spurs and England home and away, but fitting in time to watch AC Milan when he can. He is a familiar figure to travelling supporters, and his tweeted updates provided a picture of the fan experience in Qatar that eschewed the contextual controversies. For Bagley, it was just about the football. 'As a fan and especially a

————————————————

the idea of a shorter cycle for the World Cup and an enlarged World Club Championship, with 32 teams representing every Confederation (producing a possible schedule of year one, World Cup finals; year two, World Club Championship, European Championship and Coppa Libertadores; year three World Cup tournament).

Spurs fan,' he reflected, 'it was a great experience being at the Qatar World Cup. I saw 11 games and one of the best things, that we as fans will probably never experience again, was the friendly and very happy mixing of the fans, especially on the Metro system. When there were four games on every day you would see all eight groups of fans travelling on it. Every time you used the Metro or went into the large shopping mall, you would see so many fans from all of the 32 countries but mainly from Mexico, Argentina and Brazil. Even on non-matchdays they always wore their shirts. There were no issues at all with what you wore and everywhere was very clean and safe.

'I loved mixing with the other fans and really enjoyed talking to them about Spurs. The Premier League is massive and as I know from my friends in Italy, it is more popular than many domestic leagues. With Spurs having so many players with different countries it was easy to start a conversation. The Argentina fans always said 'Cuti (Romero) and Ardiles' whilst the South Korean fans were not just fans of Son but also had a real knowledge about Spurs and other Spurs players. I met South Korean Spurs fans who went to England games to support Harry Kane. I saw Richarlison score his two goals against Serbia at the magnificent Lusail Stadium and celebrated with 50,000 fans – some of them had photos with me after his brilliant second goal.'

In spite of all the surrounding controversies, Bagley's experience showed football could still provide the simplest of pleasures and the most uplifting experiences. Fond memories that will last a lifetime.

In the run-up to England's quarter-final against France, *The Guardian*'s Barney Ronay mused whether 'England are the Tottenham Hotspur of Qatar 2022.' They effected 'a good but unremarkable job' of overcoming the obstacles that had been expected but now had to subjugate the holders in order to be able to walk away with at least a degree of satisfaction of mission accomplished.

In the match against France, itself, with four minutes left to play, England were awarded a penalty, and a chance to level the scores at 2-2. Further, with momentum behind them, they looked the more ready to meet the challenge extra time would bring. Kane just needed to score. He had already scored one. And now, against the same goalkeeper he practised against in training every week, he had to do so again.

For Lloris, too, the pressure was intense. Both men knew the other's habits, preferences and foibles. And both knew the other knew. So what to do? Go against type, do something unusual, and risk not pulling it off? Or stick with the tried and tested and risk being outguessed? A relationship between club captain and vice-captain forged over years on the training field and the grounds of the Premier League had come down to an eyeball-to-eyeball confrontation between two national team captains on the world's biggest stage. To add to the pressure, a successful spot kick would see Kane become England's all-time top goalscorer. On the other hand, Lloris, appearing in a record 143rd game for France, was seeking to preserve his country's bid to become only the third holders to retain their trophy and the first since Brazil in 1962.[22]

Kane cracked, and in a replica of his miss against Eintracht Frankfurt in October, sent his penalty high over the bar. France held on for a 2-1 victory and went through to the semi-finals where they defeated Morocco, the first African country to reach this stage of the competition, 2-0.

Thankfully the vitriol directed at Marcus Rashford, Jadon Sancho and Bukayo Saka, who had missed penalties in the final of the 2020 European Championship (played a year late in 2021), was not, at least immediately, evident. (Although this pointed up the deplorable element of racism in those cases.) All the same, Kane looked broken and for Spurs spectators the thought 'what does this mean for us?' sprung to mind.

---

[22] Italy is the other nation to have retained the World Cup, in 1934 and 1938.

In the aftermath of England's exit, the question of whether the captain should have taken the second penalty was hotly debated. Without claiming to be hindsight experts, there were tweets from journalists and pundits to their colleagues accurately predicting the unfortunate turn of events. One was so sure that Kane was going to miss that he turned off the television only to switch it on seconds later to have his worst fears confirmed. But could Gareth Southgate really have instructed England's captain and talisman to relinquish responsibility at such a crucial juncture? Maybe if Jordan Henderson, the most senior player and vocal leader, had still been on the pitch he could have assessed Kane's state of mind and persuaded him to step down.

Kane does not shirk responsibility, a commendable quality that sits alongside so many more in a world-class player still not fully appreciated as he should be. But is his innate confidence in his own ability to succeed at the very top overwhelmed on occasion by doubt? It's a complex question, and one which reveals the pressure and the fine margins between success and failure that are brought to bear in elite sport.[23]

---

[23] Kane's miss was his fourth for England in 21 attempts. For Spurs he has been successful on 41 occasions at time of writing, failing seven times, which compares unfavourably with a consummate

Ian Wright, as he so often does, gave a thoughtful and insightful assessment on his *Wrighty's House* podcast. He said, 'I think it was an incredible piece of goalkeeping by Lloris, because he's thinking, 'I know you're going to go into this corner again'. And Kane is thinking 'Lloris knows that's my penalty and he's going to try and go that way again'. You know this man intimately; he knows you intimately. You train against each other five days a week. So Harry Kane's mind is thinking 'this has to be perfect, I have to put some more on it and get it higher'. I'm laying this on thick because the penalty discourse is going to be so lazy. Kane made a very smart decision under a lot of pressure, and he got it marginally off and that's it.'

So England were out and Kane, along with his club colleague Richarlison, was left to ponder what might have been.[24] Brazil had looked ominously auspicious and the Spurs striker was shaping up to be

---

penalty taker such as Matt Le Tissier who scored 47 for Southampton and missed just once.

[24] This was not the first time that a vital moment in the career of one of the Premier League's most prolific marksmen may have turned out differently had his manager been more assertive. What would have happened, for example, in the 2019 Champions League final if Mauricio Pochettino had decided Kane was not fit enough to start, but retained the option to use him from the bench?

one of the stars of a star-studded side. However, Brazil could not subdue Croatia, their quarter-final opponents, and Richarlison was substituted on 84 minutes with the score sheet still blank. Neymar looked to have settled the outcome but with three minutes of extra time remaining, Croatia equalised to take the tie to penalties. Inexplicably, Neymar was due to take the last penalty, but he never got the chance; Brazil capitulated in the shoot-out. Perišić once again proved his ability at the highest level, reprising his exploits in 2014 and 2018 to record his sixth goal along with his three assists, and the sight of Luka Modrić at 37 pulling the strings stirred the memory of how fortunate Spurs had been to benefit from his skill and technique in 160 games.

The other quarter-finals saw the curtain come down on Cristiano Ronaldo's World Cup career as Portugal were stunned by Morocco, and a humdinger between the Netherlands and Argentina – another chapter in an enduring World Cup rivalry – saw Cristian Romero make it three Spurs in the competition's penultimate round.

Argentina and France swept aside their opponents to set up a final that, for once, after a tepid first half, proved worthy of the occasion; a vibrant second period and an ever-changing extra time ending all square at 3-3. For Lloris, footballing immortality beckoned. Could he become the first man to captain his country to consecutive World Cup victories? For Romero, the ultimate glory was tantalisingly close, a prospect made more enticing because it was surely the last chance for his captain to lift the FIFA World Cup trophy, and perhaps settle once and for all the Messi-Ronaldo debate.

For many observers, the clash between Lionel Messi and Kylian Mbappe – two megastars of Qatari-owned Paris St German facing off in the World Cup final in Qatar – exemplified the objectives of sportswashing. But, after the dust had settled on an extraordinary encounter, it was football's ability to enthral and delight that was the abiding emotion. While the tournament was, according to *Le Monde*, 'a symbolic and diplomatic success for its home country', one couldn't help but wonder whether it really had been worth spending quite so many billions. Qatar had been in the spotlight, but that hadn't obscured much of what had been parked temporarily in the shadows.

The 2022 World Cup will forever be Messi's World Cup, the tournament in which he took his place on the podium alongside Maradona and Pele with seven goals and three assists, comparing favourably with Pele in 1970 and Maradona in 1986.[25] And Messi was

---

[25] A hat-trick by Kylian Mbappe, the first in a final since Geoff Hurst in 1966, topped off his eight goals, the most since his countryman Just Fontaine's 13 in 1958, and gave him the consolation prize of the Golden Boot.

perhaps the best example to encapsulate the dilemma of modern football at the highest level. To watch him play was invariably to witness skill and marvel at his technique. Yet behind the pleasure was the unease regarding the Messi industry, the extravagant wages, the tax issues, the Saudi and Qatari tie-ups. A simple game lit up by stars but made complicated by the power it gave them.

For the two Spurs on the pitch for the final act, there were very different sensations. Romero, at 24, had reached the pinnacle of the game and had a bright future ahead of him, but how much of it would be spent in north London was now open to question. For Lloris, on the other hand, it was a matter of endings and not beginnings. Error-prone for his club prior to the World Cup, just one save in the penalty shoot-out could have provided the dream ending for him.

Eight days later, the Premier League would restart, with Spurs travelling to Brentford on Boxing Day for a 12.30 kick-off to lift the curtain on the second act. Everyone was about to enter unknown territory.

9. THE BEGINNING
OF THE END

It's less than an hour to kick-off at Chiswick Park Underground station on Boxing Day. Four Spurs fans get off the train and walk through empty streets for 20 minutes before finally encountering crowds by the away entrance to the Brentford Community Stadium. With a capacity of just 17,250 – only Bournemouth's Vitality stadium is a smaller Premier League ground – and tucked away between the M4 and A205 just by Kew Bridge, it opened for business in September 2020.

Founded in 1889, seven years after Tottenham, Brentford's highest honour has been the second-tier title, and their highest league finish of fifth in the top division was attained way back in 1935/36. Overshadowed until recently by West London neighbours Fulham and Queens Park Rangers, who dismissed them when they were Championship rivals as just 'a bus stop in Hounslow', Brentford are enjoying halcyon days under the progressive and astute ownership of Matthew Benham, and had already defeated both Manchester giants in just their second Premier League season. The club's present comfortable mid-table position at this time challenges the notion that top-level, modern football is the exclusive preserve of clubs owned by... well, you know who.[26]

Comparisons can be drawn between Brentford and Brighton & Hove Albion, a club also benefiting from the consistent application of a football strategy to enjoy some of the most successful days it has ever experienced.[27] Brighton chairman Tony Bloom, like Benham, made his money from the betting market. (Benham in fact worked for Bloom until the two spectacularly fell out and Benham set up his own rival company.) Research and analysis to measure their teams' chances of creating opportunities and conceding, aligned with the professional's eye to spot trends and kinks, has enabled the two clubs to gain a place in the Premier League and then to compete with others who can draw on far superior resources.

---

[26] The use of data and statistical modelling is coupled with a painstaking search for what Brentford's head coach, Thomas Frank, calls 'good people', talent being a prerequisite but always ensured that it can be aligned with a positive attitude and hard work which produces a 'unique togetherness both on and off the pitch'.

[27] Brentford and Brighton also own sister clubs in Denmark (Midtjylland) and Belgium (Royale Union Saint-Gilloise) respectively who – by employing the same principles as their English senior counterparts – are also currently enjoying unprecedented success.

But perhaps Benham and Bloom's real achievement has been to show that football remains a sport where meritocracy can survive, despite the efforts of the big battalions to try and quash any real challenge to their pre-eminent status.

The Brentford stadium's limited capacity and the travails of Boxing Day travel for a 12.30 kick-off ensured that only 1,725 Spurs fans were in attendance. That kick-off time was at the behest of Amazon Prime, the third broadcaster in the live football market for UK-based fans. Greater competition has long been held to benefit the consumer, but once again football is an exception to the rule, a business like no other. Of the 380 games in a Premier League season, 200 are broadcast live: 128 on Sky, 52 on BT (who, as mentioned previously, also have the exclusive rights for all the UEFA club competitions) and 20 on Amazon. So, if a fan wants to see their club every time they are televised, they will need to fork out for three subscriptions which will cost around £70 a month, £815 a year, without factoring in the price of a TV licence or the associated package costs.

There are essentially two groups of fans: those who watch on the sofa or in the pub and those who go to games. For those who commit to both, their loyalty bears an additional premium. Moreover, they appear to be only valued for their entrance fees and creating the essential verisimilitude, the special atmosphere of a live event without which the astronomical rights fees paid by broadcasters would not be contemplated. Though a tiny minority of the global television audience – the Premier League is shown in 188 countries – for the most committed, the television subscriptions come on top of the costs of tickets, travel and subsistence.

The enormous rise in the cost of watching televised football has come alongside the enormous rise in attendance prices. The Premier League and its broadcast partners protest about the 'real threat' of illegal streaming. However, fans see the constant increase in charges against the billions the League earns and ask, much as their predecessors did (when huge attendances generated gate receipts that never seemed to go back into teams or stadia improvements) 'where has the money gone?' Despite a projected cost of £4 billion of wages out of an estimated Premier League revenue in 2022/23 of £6 billion, all the Big Six clubs should post an operating profit. The fans reasonably enquire when they are going to benefit? The answer – that they get great entertainment – doesn't cut it.

As the teams ran out on Boxing Day 2022 to restart the season, a lusty chorus of 'Harry Kane, he's one of our own' burst forth from the corner housing the away fans. Along with Kane, Ivan Perišić and Son Heung-Min were present, but World Cup finalists Hugo Lloris and Cristian Romero were not because, according to Antonio Conte, 'it is important to give these players a bit of rest'. Also missing as a result of World Cup injuries were Rodrigo Bentancur and Richarlison. Supporters aren't privy to what goes on at the training ground, so they cannot judge who is ready to play and who is not. Of course, a World Cup final is physically and emotionally draining, but it was eight days since the event and professional footballers rarely have an eight-day break between games. For all the legitimate concerns about overcrowded schedules, the Spurs World Cup representatives had enjoyed the benefit of a comparatively extended rest period.

Lloris was the club captain, and both he and Romero were on handsome salaries. Was it so unreasonable to expect them to get on with the job? Perišić, Son and especially Kane, all had issues of their own to deal with after their national teams had been eliminated just days before the tournament concluded, but somehow managed to put themselves in contention for a starting place. With the furore over his missed penalty, Kane could be forgiven if he was harbouring a negative thought or two about what opposition fans might have in store for him. Nevertheless, he pronounced himself 'reset and ready to go'. (After Brentford hosted Arsenal to launch the 2021/22 season, Bukayo Saka, in his first game back after his Euros penalty miss, had been spared vitriolic abuse, so maybe this was not such a bad ground at which to be making a return.)

Once more, Spurs started slowly, and it didn't take long before the home side's terrace twits piped up with a chorus of 'You let your country down' whenever Kane got near the ball, prompting a response from the visitors of 'Toney, what's the odds?', a reference to the Brentford's striker's ongoing troubles with gambling allegations. Is all fair in love and war, or is the insistence on using anything possible to get at opponents just another depressing aspect of modern football?

Japhet Tanganga, a surprise selection, played as you would expect from someone who had not featured in the first team all season, and was constantly outwitted by Ivan Toney; Fraser Forster, meanwhile, looked uncertain as Lloris's deputy. For the ninth time in the season, Spurs went behind, and they were fortunate to go in at the break only one goal down. When play resumed, Brentford soon scored a second, capitalising on awful defending after a corner had been needlessly conceded by Eric Dier, who sliced a clearance 25 yards backwards and over the line.

To make matters worse, it seemed Spurs had decided not to get their act together until the second half was well under way. After an hour, they roused themselves. Clément Lenglet delivered a perfect cross from the left for Kane – who else? – to head in on 65 minutes; his tenth Boxing Day goal marking the fact that he had now scored against all of the 32 Premier League clubs he had faced during his career. Class, character and technique in an instant. No letdown.

Davinson Sánchez replaced Tanganga, and the back line looked instantly more assured. Lenglet's offensive approach allowed Perišić to move freely across the front line. On 71 minutes, after being set up by Kulusevski, making a most welcome return, Højbjerg curled in an equaliser and Spurs looked set for another late show. They had a legitimate penalty claim turned down, and Kane headed against the bar. But victory didn't come.

Two points dropped or one salvaged? A win for Newcastle later that afternoon and, worse still, another three points for Arsenal the following day, which kept them seven points clear at the top of the table, provided the context. Conte reflected after the game that it was 'not possible' for Spurs to keep conceding first, and that it was 'important to be more stable'. Responding to the inevitable January transfer-window questions, he said, 'I think if there is the opportunity to strengthen the squad, we will do something. You know which is our policy... we will try to follow this policy and to improve the team. If there is the possibility to strengthen the squad we will do it. Otherwise, we will continue with these players, and I am happy with them.'

Pressed further on the way forward, he answered, 'You know about the signing, signing players, and about young players. About players with not big salaries. We have to sign players, that they can stay in our vision, in the vision of the club.'

So, the manager was happy with the players he had; it would be nice to sign more; the club has a policy about signing players; this is why some signings are 'club signings' with an eye to the future; he was doing the best he could in the conditions he had to work in.

But, as one Spurs fan said after this game, 'This is an example of where Conte gets on my wick. He's essentially saying he can't do the job without the best, most expensive talent bought for him, but makes it sound like he's doing us a favour. We play paint-by-numbers football in first halves and are awful. When we have to rip up the plan, the shackles come off and we actually play a bit. I really don't want to see yet another ENIC managerial failure but it's getting hard to defend Conte.'

Triggered more by Arsenal's win than Spurs' draw, any measured assessment was lost in the noise. Growing discontent with the club's owners was threatening to combine with a desperate desire to see Conte succeed to produce a combustible atmosphere. Before the club's board drew up its pricing plan for the new stadium, the Tottenham Hotspur Supporters' Trust (THST) had warned that the intention to impose some of the highest prices in Europe would increase the demands for a trophy or two and now the comment 'champagne prices for fizzy pop football' was cropping up more and more. Moreover, the ENIC out crew stepped up their social media criticism and sporadic chants echoing their stance were increasingly audible at games. Discontent with the club's board has long been a feature at Spurs, but outside of a vocal minority who showed little enthusiasm for aligning with anyone who didn't think exactly as they did, that discontent was somewhat measured.

THST had tried to get an indication of feeling about the board in its annual pre-season survey that was open to any Spurs supporter who wanted to fill it in. The result from 6,000 respondents was that just 3% agreed with the statement 'I'd like ENIC to sell up now', but 70% agreed that 'They do a great job with the business side but I'd like more focus on the football side'. While worries about whether Conte was being sufficiently backed were growing, the 70%'s view remained pretty much where most fans were, especially in the absence of any viable alternative ownership of the club.

A frequent accusation hurled at the directors is that they are reluctant to spend money. And yet ENIC had responded to complaints of their parsimony by backing their elite manager with a cash injection of £150 million to finance the purchases of Richarlison, Yves Bissouma and Djed Spence, along with transforming Cristian Romero's loan into a permanent deal at a total cost of more than £42 million. And although no fee was involved, modifying the wages policy in order to pay Ivan Perišić an annual salary of more than £8.5 million.

Was lack of absolute expenditure the issue, or was it the quality of recruitment or the absence of a clear football strategy? What had really changed in the last six months? Were the murmurings of discontent just a reaction to a few bad results, or a sign of a deeper malaise?

The first month of the new year looked ripe to deliver some answers; the start of the FA Cup campaign against Portsmouth, a transfer window with all its associated hullaballoo, and with seven games spearheaded by the crucial home derby against league leaders Arsenal.

10. DESIRE

The first encounter between Tottenham Hotspur and Arsenal as league rivals was in 1909, with Arsenal securing a 1-0 victory. Since then, there have been a further 191. Strictly speaking, the North London Derby didn't exist until 1913, after Arsenal had upped sticks from south of the river and moved in four miles down the road from Tottenham's ground in north London. And as number 193 approached, talk was of turning points, as it so often is before the derby.

It was not hard to imagine what Mikel Arteta's pre-match motivational speech would be. The ridicule directed at Arsenal for getting the corresponding fixture the previous season postponed because 'the necessary players' were not available and the subsequent humbling and deprivation of a Champions League place when the game was eventually played was deeply resented. Now, though, Arsenal were top of the league by playing the kind of attractive football Antonio Conte seemed entirely disinterested in. Backing Mikel Arteta's once much mocked 'project', the fans who had been vociferously calling for his head just a year before now serenaded him by singing 'We've got super Mik Arteta; He knows exactly what we need; Kieran at the back, Gabi in attack, Arsenal on their way to Champions League'.

Pointedly, not 'on our way to win the league'. Fans used to sing for the chance to win trophies rather than to prioritise pragmatism. This was perhaps not surprising coming from followers of a club that arguably had lost its way. Arsenal had appeared satisfied just to be in contention for the top trophies without ever really seeming that bothered about winning them. Foreign investors moved in to change the rules of engagement, leaving Arsenal's self-sufficiency strategy in their wake. The historic family dynasties– the Bracewell-Smiths succeeded by the Hill-Woods – were marginalised, replaced by an American sports entrepreneur who saw the club as just another arm of his empire. The drop in ambition suited Arsène Wenger, arguably the most successful manager in Arsenal's history, enabling him to settle into a position where no one could challenge him. And so the club drifted, as the once revolutionary genius was overtaken by others who took his ideas on board and modified them for a changing environment.

Arsenal seemed to be marking time. In Wenger's pomp they had a clear identity. Much to the annoyance of Spurs fans, they even shook off the 'Boring, Boring Arsenal' tag to become regarded as entertainers who were consistent achievers while Spurs, on the other hand, exemplified the workmanlike qualities of a mid-table Premier League occupant, at best.

Times change. Arsenal had not won a league title since 2004. European success was as elusive as ever. There had been seven FA Cup triumphs since 2002, but FA Cup wins didn't have the pedigree of bygone days, despite their usefulness in taunting Spurs, for whom one would represent a successful season, their last having come way back in 1991.

By 2018 Wenger was gone, a significant section of the club's support having called noisily for his head over a sustained period. His successor Unai Emery, harshly treated by both the media and the fans, which didn't reflect well on either party, lasted less than two seasons and Arsenal were at a standstill. Qualifying regularly for the Champions League but getting knocked out at the business end had slid away into not qualifying at all. Spurs were now the more regular competitors in Europe's top club tournament, and their swanky new stadium was opening up a financial gap on the neighbours who once looked set to disappear from view.

As the January 2023 derby approached, Spurs could look back on six years in which they had finished above Arsenal in the Premier League. But the cyclical nature of football is hard to break, and Spurs were nervous. Critics of the Tottenham board detected that same tendency – settling for just being there – that looked to have stalled Arsenal. Now their neighbours displayed not only purpose but swagger, and Spurs' form was erratic, belying their fifth place in the table. After making their best start to a Premier League season with 23 points from their first seven league fixtures, they then proceeded to concede the first goal in seven successive league matches and were in the bottom half of the table on current form.

A New Year's Day 2-0 home defeat to an improving Aston Villa side that had been flickering into life (but which rarely surpassed mediocre) had sucked what little air remained out of an already deflated atmosphere, and for the first time chants of 'We want Levy out' and 'Daniel Levy, get out of my club' could be heard loud enough for the media pack to prick up their ears. The anti-ENIC and anti-Levy chants intensified away at Crystal Palace three days later, although it was noticeable that they were most avidly taken up by younger fans who might not have been expected to have accumulated sufficient ticketing points to qualify for a London derby away ticket.

Hugo Lloris put his fumbles against Aston Villa behind him and ensured that he and his teammates reached the interval on equal terms. Then out of the blue came four second half goals, courtesy of two from Harry Kane, his 14th and 15th in the league, together with a welcome one from the hitherto misfiring Son Heung-Min and a rare one from Matt Doherty. For once, Spurs scored the first goal in a game and looked all the better for it. 'There are moments you need this kind of performance,' reflected Antonio Conte, 'and today, we did it.'

A ponderous home 1-0 third round FA Cup victory over Portsmouth – roared on by 9,000 Pompey fans – courtesy of Kane (again) brought the enticing prospect that he might break Jimmy Greaves's all-time goal-scoring record in the next home match, the second north London derby of the season. But the confidence levels of the home supporters were not elevated. The mood was fractious, with the Levy Out crowd intent on outshouting the greater number who, while harbouring misgivings about the board's priorities, nevertheless worried that they should be careful what they wished for.

Conte continued to fuel the fires and his tactics, both on and off the field, were beginning to grate. Alasdair Gold, who has diligently covered Spurs for the www.football.london website for years, reflected after the Villa game that, 'The opening day of 2023 brought a flat, miserable, hungover home defeat, a bench with not a single attacker on it, chants for the chairman to 'get out of our club' and Antonio Conte making sure everyone knew that he had informed Spurs last summer they were going to be rubbish this season... There's no doubting Conte did a great job in turning around Tottenham's fortunes last season, but he's glossing over the fact that Spurs had finished in the top four in four of the six seasons before his arrival, coming third, second and third again in a row amid those years.'

Sky decreed that the derby would be played on a Sunday as darkness squeezed out the weak afternoon sun of a cold January afternoon. While the bars on the High Road and in the stadium bounced as they always did on match day, there was apprehension about what was in prospect compounded by the ongoing skirmishes of what threatened to develop into a civil war among the home contingent. A potentially pivotal fixture, doubts about whether the board and the manager had the same vision, the timing right in the middle of a transfer window with all its associated hype led to a strong sense of foreboding.

And so it came to pass. A promising start soon proved to be a false dawn as another predictable, dysfunctional first half display panned out. Then Hugo Lloris decided to help the ball into his own net, leading to a moment of stunned silence before the away section in the northeast corner of the ground thundered out their delight. Worse was to follow as Martin Ødegaard scored when allowed too much space on the edge of the penalty box – reprising what Thomas Partey had been allowed to do earlier in the season. Alan Shearer[28] on *Match of the Day 2* summed up the match as 'A tale of two

---

[28] Alan Shearer holds the Premier League goalscoring record of 260, but assuming Harry Kane stays fit and continues his career in England, the boy from Chingford is on course to take the mantle.

goalkeepers. Lloris put his team under huge pressure. A Premier League goalkeeper shouldn't (allow the ball) to be going into the back of the net. On the other hand, the guy at the other end (Aaron Ramsdale) made some really good saves.'

True to precedent, Spurs improved in the second half but flattered to deceive against opponents brimming with confidence. As hostilities were brought to a close, the inescapable fact was that this was yet another game lost to one of the teams above them in the table. Arsenal had anticipated Conte would stick with his system and, therefore, his side would not be able to gain control of the midfield. Outnumbered, Spurs couldn't slow the pace or speed it up. 'The way Conte sets the team up tactically, it creates a negative mindset (amongst the players),' observed Danny Murphy[29] again on *Match of the Day 2*. 'There weren't enough leaders to change the dynamic. When you are that passive in the first half, you have to do something.'

Maybe Conte's thoughts were elsewhere – the recent passing of his friends and contemporaries, Siniša Mihajlović and Gianluca Vialli, on top of the sudden death of his trusted colleague Gian Piero Ventrone and the separation from his family back in

---

[29] In a 20-year career Danny Murphy made 600 senior appearances, including 28 for Spurs and nine for England.

Italy, must have affected him deeply. And perhaps his unease was contagious, reinforcing a growing feeling that he would not be at Spurs the following season. Certainly, his judgement appeared awry as he said he was pleased with the performance. He told the media, 'About the performance, I'm not disappointed. I'm not disappointed because we knew that the game could be really difficult because Arsenal is a really, really strong team. At the same time, I'm a bit disappointed for the way we lost.'

Not disappointed but, instead, disappointed. And seemingly unaware that his team was making the same mistakes over and over again. Moreover, Arsenal showed the greater desire – to prove a point, to make a statement, to put one over on the old enemy while pursuing a greater prize.

At the final whistle, Arsenal goalkeeper Aaron Ramsdale kissed his badge and pulled it out towards the hardcore Spurs support in the South Stand. He'd taken a lot of abuse from the home crowd but nonetheless it was probably best advised to resist the temptation to exchange insults. Richarlison took exception to his antics and in doing so incited a reaction as both sides piled in to practise their best gesticulative moves. Perhaps a little more passion from the home team during the preceding 90 minutes would have been more productive.

As the pantomime played out on the touchline, a fan managed to climb on to the perimeter fence and land a glancing kick on Ramsdale before disappearing back into the crowd as the watching stewards decided what it was they should be doing. It looked worse than it was, but the simple fact is you can't have players being assaulted on the pitch, and Spurs would have to hope the CCTV failures that seem so often to occur when an embarrassing incident breaks out would not add to the general misery of the afternoon for all concerned with Tottenham Hotspur.

Arsenal were now eight points clear at the top of the table and Spurs were faced with the daunting prospect of playing Manchester City away and home over the next couple of weeks. City were the only side that looked capable of overhauling the league leaders so Spurs fans faced a dilemma: hope for two wins that would surely all but hand Arsenal the title, or hope for two defeats that would all but finish off their own chances of a Champions League spot.

11. WINDOWS 23

Following the latest underwhelming performance in the derby – of all matches! – the prospect of Arsenal carrying off the Premier League title was beginning to loom uncomfortably large. Coupled with the fact that the mid-season transfer window was in full flow, all the ingredients were present for an unnerving time at Tottenham Hotspur.

Transfer windows provide a vivid illustration of how dramatically the game has changed since the formation of the Premier League. In 1996, the first Sky contract was reaching its conclusion and the new one priced domestic TV rights at £670 million – up from £191.5 million. The beneficiaries were starting to flex their muscles to entice foreign stars to these shores.[30] However, the big transfer deal of summer 1996 came when Newcastle United paid £15 million for Alan Shearer from Blackburn Rovers, beating Manchester United to his signature. The deal made him the world's most expensive footballer, costing £2.2 million more than Barcelona paid PSV Eindhoven for 'O Fenomeno' – the original Ronaldo. Elsewhere, Parma signed Lilian Thuram for £4.5 million, and a certain Zinedine Zidane joined

---

[30] Tottenham Hotspur's turnover in 1996/1997 (14 months) was £27.4 million. In 2021/2022 (12 months) it was £444 million.

Juventus for the princely sum of £3.2 million. Nowadays, those figures are more likely to be the monthly wage of anyone at the top end of the market.

Back then, transfers could transpire at any time up until 31 March and the newcomer would be drafted straight into the team. In 2002/03, the regulations were changed so that players could be signed only during set periods in July, August and January. The restrictions were introduced after legal wrangling over contracts, prompted by the European Commission. Much of the argument centred around the balance between contractual stability and freedom of movement, and the compromise solution was the introduction of summer and winter transfer periods.

In the Premier League's own words, 'The alternative was to bring football in line with most other industries where contracts were not enforceable or liable for appropriate compensation, i.e. notice periods being served and players moving at will. The football authorities across Europe felt this would fatally undermine the footballing economy and remove the incentive for clubs to invest in developing players.' What wasn't considered was the important difference between first- and second-class citizens. Did it really make sense to treat elite athletes on top contracts in the same way as their lesser brethren?

Monied clubs had always deployed their financial muscle to attract the best players. Spurs, for example, would traditionally make one star signing every season to augment their team and generate box office interest. Jimmy Greaves was one such example, signed for a record fee as the only player that manager Bill Nicholson thought could improve his Double-winning team. And, down the years, Spurs have signed many a top talent – Alan Gilzean, Martin Chivers, Ralph Coates, Ossie Ardiles and Ricky Villa, Steve Archibald and Garth Crooks, Clive Allen, Chris Waddle, Paul Gascoigne and Teddy Sheringham, who were expensively acquired and who subsequently became club heroes. However, what's changed is scale and expectation. Today, their fees appear ludicrously minuscule. Gascoigne, the most gifted young player in England at the time, was signed for £2 million from Newcastle United in July 1988. In January 2023, the lowest disclosed fee paid by a Premier League club was the £3 million Gazza's old club stumped up for West Ham United's 21-year-old defender Harrison Ashby, who had just seven minute's experience of the top flight.[31]

---

[31] 85% of the Premier League's transfer spending went overseas, a sum without which some of the European leagues could not survive in their present form. Serie A and La Liga cast envious and resentful eyes at the riches of the Premier League, which served to strengthen the determination of their

For many supporters, doing deals is the measure of your club's ambition. If they are bigger or better than your rivals, or if there are more of them, then you've stolen a march on the opposition. Lack of activity is regarded as a missed opportunity. The connection between the need to address an issue and the compulsion to *do a deal* seems to have become obscured in all the media frenzy as deadline day looms.

A transfer 'rumour' can be run with relatively little sourcing or attribution – just get a name and a club in the headline and the audience will follow in their thousands on social media and Sky Sports News. Stories are simultaneously runnable and plausibly deniable. And it all culminates in a gala programming orgy of Deadline Day's live coverage on every broadcast medium.

There is a voracious appetite for deals. Transfers demonstrate ambition, cachet, heft. Apparently, football can be viewed as a trading card game, with clubs stockpiling talent to prevent competition

---

leading lights to establish a European Super League, initially ostracising the English, as the only means of challenging the financial dominance of the Premier League. (Of the 10 richest clubs in the world, six – Manchester City, Liverpool, Manchester United, Chelsea, Tottenham Hotspur, and Arsenal – come from the Premier League).

getting their hands on it and only worrying about how best to utilise it later. It is a long way indeed from the days when transfers were seen primarily in football terms. Like players, coaches – at the top level – are now rewarded handsomely for their scarcity value and (unlike players) there is no embargo on securing them. And yet it seems that the more 'elite' the coach, the less coaching he is required to do. Bringing players through, unearthing and developing prospects, making the whole greater than the sum of the parts, that's yesterday's scenario. Today, an elite coach demands the best players are delivered to him twice a year, so naturally their costs rise exponentially.

And it is all so much more frenetic in the winter window. The time period is more concentrated. The pattern of the season has already begun to unfold, together with the fact that the situation, for better or worse, in just four months' time may be radically different. It all ensures business is intrinsically complicated. Significant deals are done in January, but immediate returns on investment are harder to come by.

At Spurs, the failure to acquire anyone at all in 2018/19 still rankles. The club was the first Premier League club to do no business during a window since the system began. The opportunity to move up a gear had been evident for some time except, it seems, to the club's board, whose explanation for the lack of activity was that none of the available targets within their budget would be an improvement on the existing personnel. Manager Mauricio Pochettino disagreed and called for 'new furniture' to enhance fittingly the splendid new house of Spurs, and emphasised the need for a 'painful rebuild'. His words went unheeded and six months after he uttered them, he was gone, dismissed so abruptly that he had to leave his goodbyes to the players he had taken so far over five and a half years on a whiteboard at an empty training ground.

Pochettino was seemingly unaware that he wouldn't get the backing he wanted; the players picked up on this and the club began to stagnate. Appointing José Mourinho as his successor was supposed to reverse the process and show immediate progress, but his approach went against everything the club traditionally stood for and which Pochettino had put in place. Maybe Daniel Levy failed to appreciate how damaging such a sudden and total strategic change could be.

Spurs had thrown away the chance to build on what Pochettino achieved, replacing a manager who wanted the best for the club with a manager who perhaps only wanted the best for himself. Mourinho's first instinct was to deflect rather than face up to inherited issues. 'Same coach, different players,' was his response when asked why he couldn't do at Spurs what he had done so spectacularly elsewhere. He had a point, but the football was uninspiring, the man-management worse, and within 17 months he had departed.

Antonio Conte had been identified perhaps as the more modern version of Mourinho – a successful coach who had moved with the times. Initially, Levy had failed to hire him, and Spurs inexplicably stumbled through four months with Nuno Espirito Santo, before Conte could be persuaded to give London another try. He was clearly a manager who wanted the finished article, brought in to execute his long-standing productive system. There was no long-term project, just a drive to win. That suited many fans, as long as it succeeded.

Conte knew he was in a position to assert leverage on the board to get what he wanted. The summer window of 2022 was a step in the right direction, but it was evident that more was needed in January: a right wing-back, a central defender – preferably one who could play on the left – and more options up front wouldn't go amiss. Once again, the transfer window pressure was on, and the question of how aligned the board and the manager were was to the fore.

*

Back on the field of play, there was the small matter of a visit to league champions Manchester City after the ignominy of the derby debacle. 'What better fixture could there be?' the world-weary Spurs fans ironically asked.

Inconsistency showed its positive face, however, with the visitors putting in a disciplined first-half performance and snatching two goals – including one from the most unlikely source of Emerson Royal – to reach the break leading 2-0. But from the moment Julian Alvarez pulled one back in the 51st minute, Spurs looked forlorn; confidence drained away along with discipline, and City's 4-2 victory was the conclusion. The only consolation was that City had kept up the pressure on Arsenal at the top of the table.

*

Four days later, at Craven Cottage, the 'Levy Out' chants were louder than ever. Spurs ground out a much-needed 1-0 result courtesy of Kane again to stop the slide, providing the away end – which had gone through the entire songbook in a magnificent show of support – something to smile about at last.

It was hard not to imagine the watching Spurs directors gritting their teeth as their club's fans serenaded 'Antonio, Antonio, Antonio' despite watching the deadly dull fare that had been served up. Conte, surely, should have been able to extract more from a front line of Kane, Son and Kulusevski?

*

Once again the January days went by and Spurs had not made a move, aside from snatching Villareal's Dutch forward Arnaut Danjuma from under the noses of Everton. It was the sort of blow that usually befell Spurs as they dillied and dallied to try and squeeze the maximum from any negotiation. In as far as it showed they were capable of acting decisively, it was a welcome move. However, with Bryan Gil leaving on loan in the other direction, Danjuma's arrival didn't increase selection choices.

The focus of attention was centred on Sporting Lisbon's right wing-back Pedro Porro, who, it was said, was essential for Conte's system to work well, and who the club had tried to sign in the summer. The media reported Porro to be the club's number one target, but eight days before the deadline, an agreement seemed as far off as ever. Yet again, it was all going to the eleventh hour. Had the summer's relative decisiveness been an aberration rather than a sign of good things to come?

One obstacle that might have been in the way of progress was a large question mark over Fabio Paratici, the man who was intrinsically involved in transfer activity at his previous employer. A long-running investigation by the Italian authorities had resulted in him receiving a 30-month ban from Italian football as part of a number of sanctions on Juventus executives for false accounting. It was unclear whether the ban would be extended, but the suspension contained a request to make it applicable to all UEFA and FIFA members.

Juventus announced its intention to appeal, making it difficult for anyone to arrive at a definitive conclusion but, with the sword of Damocles poised over Paratici's head, it was an uneasy situation for his current employers, not least because it evaded the issue of how willing other clubs would be to do business with someone tainted by involvement in dubious transfer activities. No comment on the matter was forthcoming from the Spurs board, which fuelled further speculation and uncertainty.

*

During ENIC's tenure, Spurs has spent £1.933 billion on transfers, according to Goal.com. Figures compiled by Football Observatory and quoted by Sky put net spending in the 10 years from 2012 at £282 million, placing Spurs 16th in the table of top European club spenders and 10th among Premier League clubs, below West Ham, Everton and Aston Villa.

Critics of the club's reluctance to spend – according to their means and beyond – felt vindicated, despite the evidence of how much trouble this has got others into in the past. Nevertheless, a low net spend sends a signal that owners are less prepared to put their hands in their pockets than they are to ask the fans to fork out increasing amounts for tickets and merchandise. As the Supporters' Trust had pointed out, when you chose to charge some of the highest prices in Europe, people expect you to spend accordingly, whatever the business logic.

For years, Spurs sat far behind the top clubs when total wage bills were totted up. In 2017, when England international Danny Rose publicly blasted the wage policy (and was fined for doing so), the top earners were paid substantially less than those in similar positions at other clubs. Rose, for example, was on half the wage of Manchester United's Luke Shaw, and Mousa Dembélé was on a comparative pittance compared to Paul Pogba, admittedly United's highest-paid player.

The criterion for a healthy financial club is the wages-to-turnover ratio, and Spurs has consistently posted one of the lowest in the Premier League. However, with the return of fans to the stadium after the Covid-19 hiatus, there were significant increases in matchday and commercial income, enabling all staff remuneration to be substantially increased whilst easily complying with the regulatory financial restrictions of the Premier League and UEFA. Tottenham Hotspur was now a bigger club than Arsenal, ahead of their neighbours in all key revenue sources – matchday, commercial and broadcasting. Yet Arsenal sat comfortably looking down on them from the top of the league, which might suggest the quality of the decision-making, rather than the size of the spend, is what should be questioned.

At key moments, most notably under Harry Redknapp and Pochettino, the board seemed to have forgotten that To Dare was To Do. And whilst Levy had played his transfer cards right when he held all the aces (as in the case of Gareth Bale), the odds, it seemed, needed to be stacked in his favour before he could conclude those famously hard-headed deals.

Levy's experience with Luka Modrić may have changed his strategy. The chairman had turned down a princely deadline-day offer in the belief that the midfield maestro would help Spurs achieve Champions League qualification that season. The prize did not materialise, and Modrić was eventually sold to Real Madrid for a sum considerably short of the offer previously received. Levy was not prepared to miss out again.

Bought from Southampton in 2007, Bale struggled to establish himself as the first-choice left-back due to the impressive form of Benoît Assou-Ekotto. More regular appearances followed when Assou-Ekotto was injured and, when he regained fitness, manager Harry Redknapp moved Bale further forward in order to accommodate both of them. By chance, Bale had found his *métier*. He immediately flourished with virtuoso displays, highlighted by his single-handed demolition of Internazionale in the Champions League. That performance alone attracted worldwide attention, and his scintillating form continued, with 21 goals in 33 Premier League games in 2012/13, and both the Players and Football Writers' Player of the Year title. He was offered, and signed, a new four-year deal in 2010.

Now, incredibly, the hottest property in world football, it was inevitable that Bale would leave for greener pastures. Levy persuaded Jonathan Barnett, Bale's agent, to get his client to sign a contract extension until 2015. With over two years remaining, Levy could negotiate from a position of strength. It is in these situations where the chairman is at his best – selling to a bigger, wealthier club that prioritises trophies, and is able to push them to the limit. In September 2013, Real Madrid paid Tottenham Hotspur a world record fee of £85.1 million for Bale.

A similar satisfactory outcome was achieved with the sale of Kyle Walker to Manchester City in July 2017. A long-term contract until 2019 enabled Levy to extract another world record fee of £50 million for a defender.

Perhaps emboldened by the Bale and Walker episodes, and forgetting the precedent of the Modrić transaction, Levy missed other opportunities to sell at the top of the market and by the time Rose and Deli Alli left the club, arguably millions had been forfeited.

Moreover, when the boot is on the other foot and Spurs are the wealthier suitors, it's a different story. For example, they were forced to pay their most expensive fee ever – £55.5 million with a possible further £9 million – for Tanguy Ndombele, thanks to the equally tough negotiating skills of Jean-Michel Aulas, the President and owner of Olympique

Lyonnais. Unfortunately, the France international failed to make an impact in England and was deemed expendable by both Mourinho and Conte. Ndombele plied his trade on loan and thrived with Serie A Napoli.

Applying Oscar Wilde's definition of a cynic – a person 'who knows the price of everything and the value of nothing' – to Levy is palpably unfair. More to the point, it could be said that Levy knows the best price but his judgement on value can occasionally be awry. All the same, big transfer fees don't guarantee prosperity, something Levy delights in pointing out to his critics. Of the club's most expensive signings since 2012, only Moussa Dembélé, who cost £17.1 million, and Son Heung-Min, signed for £27 million, can be said to have been unqualified successes, which of course begs the question of why millions have been wasted on countless others? No wonder, then, that the squad has often appeared stacked with deadwood that the business maestros on the board cannot move on at a price they're prepared to take. Cue successive managers' perennial complaints that they didn't have the resources they needed.

Asking former chairmen and directors to pay substantial five-figure sums to retain their seats in the directors' box and boardroom (many chose not to do so) could be viewed as another innovative source of income when there are plenty of rich punters with no connection to the club, except in some cases as fans, waiting in line to take their place. However, what it says about the way a club should behave towards those whose spell in charge helped guide it to trophies may be interpreted as yet further evidence that money is the priority.

*

The recruitment strategy was about as clear as the steely grey and rainswept evening that greeted Spurs for their next fixture… an FA cup fourth round tie at Preston.

Despite the best efforts of the weather and the BBC, who had decided on a Saturday 6pm kick-off, a frisson of anticipation around the competition still remained. Walking to a ground and navigating unfamiliar streets by a glimpse of the floodlight pylons still stirs memories, and this was a tie that pitted (in Football League nomenclature) the old aristocrats against the *nouveau riche*.

The home fans in the corner, to the left of the 5,600-strong away contingent, displayed a banner proclaiming Preston North End as 'The Original Lilywhites', and of course Preston had been a power in the game when Spurs were just getting started. The story, without foundation, had persisted for years that Spurs had chosen white shirts in tribute to the famous Preston 'Invincibles' who became the first team to win the league and FA Cup in the same season in 1888/89. (Spurs, of course, became the first to win the modern Double in 1960/61, seemingly further underlining the connection). But Spurs actually adopted the white shirt in 1898, some 10 years after Preston's milestone and when their fortunes were beginning to wane. The same year, Spurs became a limited company, thus ensuring there was sufficient money in the coffers to buy a club kit rather than rely on the players to turn up with a suitable shirt. White had the advantage of being commonly available, and also not registered as first choice by any other club in the Southern League. (The misconception seems to have arisen from a line in the local *Weekly Herald* newspaper which read, 'The Spurs will this year wear the famous Preston North End colours, viz snow-white shirts and navy blue knickers'.) Three years later, in 1901, Spurs gained renown by becoming the first, and only, non-league team to win the FA Cup; their achievement amplified by the presence of newsreel cameras at the final tie for the first time. The plucky non-leaguers in the lilywhite shirts became an early media sensation, and their kit was firmly established in the collective consciousness.

Deepdale, a traditional ground with four separate stands tucked tight around the playing surface, was sold out. During the day, visiting fans had been made welcome in pubs and restaurants throughout the town, a stark contrast to the over-zealous restrictions imposed in supposedly grander European cities. The police approach, led by Paul Elliott, one of the best and most progressive dedicated football officers, was based on behaviour not reputation, which simply ensured fans would be supervised and not hounded. And it worked. This was one of the most friendly and enjoyable days out, despite the weather and the long, late trip home.

The first half, though, undermined the good mood somewhat; a dull and attritional affair that made Spurs fans progressively more nervous as the minutes ticked by. Preston wasn't offering much, but it would only take one goal and the visitors would be under pressure once more. Early in the second half, though, Son curled in a beauty to send any doubts packing. He added another on 69 minutes, equally emphatic in its execution, before debutant Danjuma scored a third.

Dreams of a cup run were put on hold, though, as news emerged over the rest of the weekend that the Porro deal, widely reported to be a *fait accompli*, was on the point of collapsing. It appeared that despite the long process of seduction, contractual issues began to trickle out. (Negotiation, bloody hell, as Sir Alex Ferguson might have said.) A tense final 24 hours ensued, before a resolution was found, which involved just the kind of last-minute manoeuvre with which the Spurs hierarchy like to be associated.

The deal was structured as a loan with an obligation to buy, enabling Sporting to organise club finances as they needed to, and Spurs to get their man straight away, rather than having to wait until the summer and possibly pay much more. However, there was a final twist in the tale. Hours before the window closed, it was announced that Spurs were terminating Matt Doherty's contract with immediate effect so that he could sign for Atlético Madrid. To make room for Porro, another player classed as 'non-locally-trained' had to be unloaded. Doherty was set to leave on a loan when it was discovered that the maximum number allowed in a season under FIFA rules had already been reached, hence the necessity to release him.

As a loanee, then, Porro could not be procured, so Spurs were left with the difficult choice – lose Porro and keep Doherty or lose the loan fee for Doherty and obtain Porro. They insisted no mistake had been made and everything had gone according to plan, but it was inconceivable that the club would have let a valuable asset – one they had paid £10 million for, less than two years previously – leave for nothing unless they had to. Agreement with Sporting was finally announced 10 minutes before the deadline. At least the tradition of last-minute deals was being upheld, but at what cost?

Football.London's Alasdair Gold observed, 'Spurs already had Tanguy Ndombele, Giovani Lo Celso, Sergio Reguilón, Bryan Gil, Harry Winks, Joe Rodon, Dejan Spence and Destiny Udogie out on loan. From that alone, it's worth noting that the club's transfer policies have been so poor and their ability to sell players so bad that they have seven signings that cost them around £215 million sitting out on loan at other clubs.'

So, it was a case of two in, Pedro Porro and Arnaut Danjuma, and five out, Matt Doherty and Adam Hayton to Atlético Madrid and Barnsley, respectively, and loanees Djed Spence to Rennes, Bryan Gil to Sevilla, and Harvey White to Derby. A small step forward, perhaps, but hardly the quantum leap needed to reinvigorate the squad.

Loan fees and add-ons aside, Tottenham Hotspur, along with Brentford, Everton and Manchester United, spent nothing. Nevertheless, the Premier League registered a record total January spend of £815 million, a total £2.8 billion across the two 2022/23 transfer windows. Chelsea, alone, spent £327 million; £180 million more than the total amount of the other 'Big Five' and more than La Liga, the Bundesliga, Serie A and Ligue 1 combined. Their free-spending brought their season total to over £600 million, including the British record transfer fee for Enzo Fernandez from Benfica for £106 million, and seven others (all under 22 years of age).[32] How such an influx of talent can be

---

[32] That Chelsea was able to spend so freely and keep within the rules – the Premier League allows £105 million losses over three years and UEFA a spending cap of 90% of total revenue (reduced to 80% in 2024 and 70% in 2025) – is down to amortization, the

accommodated and whether it can pay dividends in the short term must be doubtful. The optimum strategy, surely, lies somewhere in the middle ground between Chelsea's extravagance and Spurs' relative parsimony.

---

facility to spread the cost of hiring over the length of the contract. So, if a player is bought for £100 million and given an eight-year contract, only £12.5 million is the annual reported cost. Similarly, with losses; Timo Werner was bought for £47.5 million and sold back to RB Leipzig for £25 million but his two years in west London allowed amortization of £9 million, so the reported loss was only £16 million. As the Werner case shows, it is a high-risk strategy. There will inevitably be mistakes, in which case Chelsea could be stuck with a dud on high wages for years. This ability to stockpile talent worried UEFA who immediately reduced the amortization period to a maximum of five years. Whether Chelsea profitably exploited a loophole remains to be seen.

12. TO SPEND OR NOT TO SPEND

All was not well with Antonio Conte. Firmly in the eye of a storm of discontent and suspicion, still grieving from the deaths of three close friends, he had been struck down with severe stomach pains, diagnosed as having cholecystitis and taken into hospital for surgery to remove his gall bladder. After the surgery was carried out in Italy on the 2nd of February, his doctor advised him to take some time away from his duties. So, when Spurs faced Manchester City three days later, Cristian Stellini was on the touchline and Conte on the end of a phone.

Memories of the sudden collapse in Manchester a couple of weeks previously were still painful, and for some demoralised fans, hampering City's pursuit of Arsenal was as vital as what seemed to be far-fetched hopes of picking up three points. However, as Chuck Berry reminds us, 'You never can tell'. With 15 minutes on the clock, Pierre-Emile Højbjerg intercepted a wayward pass from Rodri and drove into the penalty box before laying the ball off to Harry Kane. The striker dropped off his man into space and drilled the ball first time into the bottom left-hand corner of the net in front of the South Stand. It was his 267th goal for Tottenham Hotspur – one more than the club's hitherto all-time top goalscorer, Jimmy Greaves.

Kane's face was a picture of delight as he ran, arms outstretched, to take the plaudits of the crowd and his teammates. There were tears in older eyes and smiles of pure joy everywhere. And the noise, always the noise, the guttural roar of acclimation giving way to the lusty serenade of 'He's one of our own'. And applause, applause, applause. The screens at all four corners of the stadium danced with specially-prepared graphics – a most modern of football celebrations. Broadcaster Danny Kelly never thought he would see his hero's record surpassed. 'It was something I will remember forever,' he said. 'There it was. Bang. It was happening before my eyes by a player I have nothing but admiration for.' Writing in *The Guardian*, David Hytner noted, 'It is very rare anything checks the flow of a big Premier League game. This was one such moment.'

Many believed, like Kelly, that Greaves's record was unbreakable because loyalty and longevity aren't prioritised these days. His 266 goals came in 379 games, Kane's in 416. The spurious arguments about who was the greatest would continue, of course, but what both players engendered was the thrilling anticipation of what was to come whenever a chance presented itself… the almost certain feeling the ball was destined for the back of the net. That is why they are both so cherished.

For those who had the privilege to watch Greaves play live, there is no debate, and statistics bear them out. A teenage prodigy, Greaves scored 124 top-flight goals in 157 appearances for Chelsea before he was 21, 9 in 10 Serie A games in his short stay in Milan, and 44 in 57 internationals for England. Kane is a different hero for different times, certainly more than just a lethal finisher. Yet, with 200 top-flight goals, he now sat third in the list of all-time Premier League scorers behind Wayne Rooney on 208 and Alan Shearer on 260.[33]

Can that pleasure be put aside in favour of a crude trophy count? Of course winning matters, but maybe the rare good fortune of watching two of the greatest goalscorers apply their artistry on behalf of your club matters more. In Greaves's case, it wasn't a question of either/or as his contribution to the victorious European Cup Winners and FA Cup teams testifies.

The 3,000 City fans in the northeast corner were possibly not quite as enamoured with the proceedings, but to reprise the words of renowned commentator Barry Davies, 'frankly, who cares?'[34]

---

[33] Maybe so, but in terms of top flight goals and Spurs legends, there is still some distance to travel. There are 26 players including such luminaries as Dixie Dean, Nat Lofthouse, and Ian Rush who have each scored more than 200 goals before the top of the list, the incomparable Jimmy Greaves with 357, is reached.

[34] 'Where, oh where were the Germans? And frankly, who cares?' were the words uttered by Barry Davies

As the game resumed, it was clear this had been a watershed moment. Spurs' performance was measured and controlled. Eric Dier stepped forward to deny City's midfield space, Højbjerg thwarted their attempts to take control, and Emerson Royal, for once, did not provide any ammunition for his critics. At the end, Spurs were well worth the 1-0 scoreline that few had forecast. Further, the rare display of energy and ambition raised the question of how much, if at all, Conte's absence was affecting the team, even though he was still communicating with his coaching staff as he watched from afar.

*

Before the next game at Leicester, Spurs published financial results for 2021-22. Though not greeted with the enthusiasm of the launch of the new kit, the accounts are eagerly awaited as money – or lack of it – will determine the playing strategy. The results gave a chance to assess the balance between the business and sporting objectives at the heart of the tension that was increasingly coming to define Tottenham Hotspur FC. In January, the club's Supporters' Trust had again asked the board to set out its vision. Now there was *prima facie* evidence – published, as was

---

on BBC television as Imran Sherwani scored the third goal to secure the hockey Olympic gold medal for Britain at the 1988 Seoul Olympics for the first time since 1920.

becoming a habit, as late as possible to comply with requirements – on which to arrive at a fair judgement on the way of the world in N17.

The club's total revenue was £444 million, up by 23% on the previous year and the fifth-highest in England, largely as a result of fans returning to the stadium, leading to an increase of more than £100 million on matchday and £32 million on commercial revenues; both at a record high. The two chief sponsorships with AIA, £40 million, and kit supplier Nike, £30 million, were extended to 2027 and 2033, respectively. Merchandising and other events – NFL, boxing, rugby league and union – also contributed significantly.

The record high commercial revenue of £183 million was, however, well short of Manchester City's £309 million. The level of City's commercial income had prompted suspicion that the value of sponsorship deals with entities linked to the owners had been inflated in order to get around rules on financial control. Those suspicions were thrust centre stage when the Premier League sensationally tabled a list of more than 100 alleged breaches of financial regulations against their champions, including accusations of overstating revenue and understating costs, especially with regard to managers' and players' salaries, and of a lack of cooperation in providing the information requested. Some saw the timing as an attempt by the Premier League to prove, before the publication of the much postponed but now imminent government White Paper on the governance of the English game, that it could handle issues it had shown little willingness to question, previously.

Those in charge of the league seemed not to care where money was coming from, or how it was being generated, as long as it kept coming. This pre-emptive strike looked like a last throw of the dice. If so, it not only served to underline the extent of the delusion that existed at the top of the game but also a certain tactical ineptitude. What the Premier League had done was to raise the possibility that the accomplishments of the most successful team in its competition over the last 10 years had been built on bending the rules. Would this turn out to be football's Ben Johnson moment?[35] The prognosis was not good for City as they had already been fined by UEFA in 2014, and the Court of Arbitration for Sport (CAS) in 2019, for financial contraventions.

With the Premier League allegations going back to 2008 and City robustly responding that they would answer them, it was inevitable that the process would take some time before reaching its conclusion. This

---

[35] Following Ben Johnson's world-record-breaking 100 metres victory in the 1988 Seoul Olympics, he was found to have taken anabolic steroids and failed the mandatory drugs test. He was stripped of the gold medal and banned from the sport for two years.

didn't stop speculation on how a guilty verdict might be applied, with huge fines, deduction of points, or a ban from UEFA competitions, all floated as possibilities.

Spurs, on the other hand, faced no such trauma. There was already more than €60 million in the coffers for reaching the last 16 of the Champions League and along with income from a new broadcast agreement, the club should see another jump in revenue – perhaps topping £500 million for the first time when the 2022/23 accounts are published. (However, the absence of money from Europe, which in the last five years amounted to more than €250 million will be felt in 2023/24.)

The downside was that, like most Premier League clubs, Spurs recorded a post-tax loss, in their case of £50 million. Though substantial, this was negligible compared to some of their European rivals such as PSG (£327 million), Juventus (£212 million), Internazionale (£124 million), Barcelona (£157 million) and Real Madrid (£119 million). Those losses almost certainly explain why all those clubs, apart from PSG, are proactive agitators behind the European Super League project. A main contributor to the Spurs' deficit are the interest payments of £22 million on the £1.2 billion cost of the new stadium. At £853 million, Spurs carry the highest amount of debt in the Premier League, but it is not the amount (huge though it is), more whether it can be managed that is key to sustainability. With the majority of interest payments at fixed rates spread over 20 years, as long as Spurs remain in contention for a European place, the debt will be affordable.

The club's chief expenditure was, of course, on player wages which amounted to £209 million, with a wages-to-turnover ratio of 46%, the lowest in the Premier League. A sign of a well-run business certainly, but at the expense of ambition, perhaps? No such restraint in the boardroom, with Daniel Levy again the highest-paid director in the league on remuneration of £3.3 million, up a cool half a million on the previous year. It could be argued that this was justified by qualification for the Champions League, although there would be plenty prepared to take issue with that reasoning. What cannot be denied is that Levy had overseen a remarkable business transformation, and most obviously masterminded the stadium project that had so transformed the club's finances. But trophies, there were none.

Levy's explanation in his introduction to the accounts was that, 'Our aim has always been to combine the financial stability of the club with remaining competitive on the pitch. We have to do what is right for us and sustainable in the long-term.' Further, he emphasised the obstacles the club had to overcome, 'We are competing in a league in which we have seen increased sovereign ownership and consortia finance, and in a league where the spending power is now vested in the hands of the few who dominate and have the ability to distort the market.'

All the same, he is facing up to the price of success, with £160 million spent on acquiring Richarlison, Bryan Gil, Emerson Royal, Rodrigo Bentancur, and Pape Matar Sarr and, since the accounts closed, another £76 million on Cristian Romero, Yves Bissouma, Destiny Udogie, and Djed Spence.

Of course, in the final analysis, it is not the amount of expenditure but whether it has been spent wisely that is of paramount importance, and Levy admitted, 'We have felt, and continue to feel, the financial impact of supporting player purchases which have not worked out as planned.' The increased expenditure notwithstanding, the commitment to winning titles or trophies was notably absent.

Tucked away in the notes to the statement was another important reference. Attached to the much-publicised injection of funds from ENIC was a device called a warrant that would enable the owners to subscribe for ordinary shares in the club. The warrant could only be converted in the event of a change of control, which would equate to '5% of the fully diluted capital at the point of issue'. In simple terms, this would entitle ENIC to a further stake in the club in the event of a takeover.

Michael Green, a corporate finance expert who also serves as the Supporters' Trust's financial analyst, commented that this procedure was 'dilutive of minority shareholders and, I suspect, will result in ENIC owning over 90% of shares, triggering a mandatory buy-out of minority shareholdings. If so, it's designed to clear the way for a sale. Any buyer will be purchasing 100% and won't have to think about minority shareholders.'

*

A return to Premier League action brought a shambolic 4-1 defeat to a Leicester City side who were flirting with the relegation zone. Spurs had gone ahead through Bentancur but lost their heads as the home side went on the rampage. It could even have been worse, as Harvey Barnes had a goal harshly ruled out by VAR, although he managed to score from a similar situation a few minutes later. To cap it all, Bentancur, along with Pierre-Emile Højbjerg, the mainstay of Spurs' midfield, departed with a ligament injury that would rule him out for the rest of the season.

Conte had been present on the sidelines, but was clearly not well, and not just because of the dire fare he had been forced to witness. A return to the family home was on the cards, but the trip would be made in conjunction with one to the San Siro as Tottenham resumed their pursuit of the Champions League trophy against AC Milan.

13. ENDGAME?

The return of the Champions League provided a chance to leave Premier League travails behind for a time and try to reignite the season, while also presenting Antonio Conte with the opportunity to improve on his indifferent record in the knockout stages. In turn, the truly committed could look forward to the joys of travelling away to support the team in Italy – with all the attendant hassle. Contrary to the advice given to most tourists (because of the risk of robbery), Spurs' fans would need to carry their passports so they could be verified at the ground. Supporters' groups' objections were overruled as the Italian authorities insisted it was a legal requirement, notwithstanding the fact it is unnecessary for other visitors.

There was consternation, too, when Milan officials announced that the 4,350 Spurs fans would have to be admitted through a single gate and would be required to arrive hours before the start. To ease the flow, they would be held in a secure pen. A potential recipe for disaster was only averted when more entry points were eventually made available on the morning of the match.

At least getting to the ground would be easier than on previous visits, as there was now a metro station adjacent to the stadium. Or so you might think. Hours before the game, packed carriages of fans arrived at their destination but were then sent on a long trek around a loop that took them into a car park by the away entrance – a 20-minute walk to end up where you started! Passing through one section even involved navigating a closed barrier.

Most fans took well over an hour to get in and, after climbing the circular ramps inside the stadium's iconic towers, to the very top of the Curva Nord, they arrived in their £59 seats to find facilities for which 'basic' is too kind a word. Not all the toilets were open, and those that were amounted to no more than holes in the ground. In one block, there was no light at all, leaving people to stumble around on urine-soaked floors. Women had to work out how to loosen clothing, crouch, and keep cubicle doors shut while holding mobile phone torches as people blundered about.

Seating was a free-for-all, with a minority able to claim their allotted seats and the front central rows overcrowded. At the limited number of refreshment points, there was no alcohol on sale, and other purchases could only be made by first queuing for a ticket and then queuing again to collect your item. As with the circuitous route from the Metro, there had been no advance warning to mitigate procedural discomfort.

For too long, the wretched experiences of travelling fans have been dismissed as unfortunate one-offs, but the evidence is of a systemic problem.

The previous day, the long-awaited report into the shambles of the 2022 Champions League Final in Paris had been published, and it damned UEFA and the French organisers. Once more, the finger of blame had initially been pointed at the fans, only for them to be exonerated as innocent victims. The culpabilities of the authorities, who had apologised for their behaviour, had long been known, yet it had no bearing on the Spurs fans' miserable episode. The contrast with the Ultras in the Curva Sud making a terrific racket and festooning their stand with banners and tifo displays was extreme. There were three huge messages tailored for this Valentine's Day encounter: 'You are my only love', 'I live only for you', and 'I will never betray you'.

Doug Bagley had travelled to the game with his Spurs mates, but also to meet up with his Milan friends – he had been a member of the Milan Ultras group *Fossa Dei Lioni* – and had watched Milan over 150 times. Before the game, Bagley had posted advice about how to make the most of the city and its fan culture. Asked if 'Ultras' meant 'hooligans', he rebuffed the assumption, 'No, it certainly does not. Unfortunately, that is the understanding in many countries, including England. The Ultras groups are organised and help fans travel to away games and represent the most loyal fans in the stadium. They are one big family. But they will protect the family.'

Bagley also provided some perspective regarding the conditions faced by the away contingent. The top tier, Tier 3, of the San Siro went right around the ground and in the Curva Sud the home fans had to put up with 'the same terrible toilet facilities. Of course, they are unacceptable for all fans.' The police, he said, 'generally treat all away fans as if they are hooligans' because of past incidents such as having to deal with Napoli fans on the rampage and when Dinamo Zagreb turned up with an away contingent described as '3,900 fighting men'. Not surprisingly then, as Bagley explained, 'The politicians and police are becoming stricter in their methods and the restrictions they apply to all fans – especially away fans – and not just the troublemakers. What happened with the Spurs fans was unacceptable, but the Milan fans suffer similar treatment at most away games in Italy.' Football, eh?

On the pitch, Spurs also had to cope with unfavourable circumstances. With Pierre-Emile Højbjerg suspended and Rodrigo Bentancur and Yves Bissouma injured, only Oliver Skipp and Pape Mata Sarr were available to fill the midfield slots. In the event, they acquitted themselves well, and Spurs were marginally the better of two mediocre sides. After going ahead at seven minutes, Milan were content to sit on their lead and found it easy to contain the visitors. With Harry Kane, Son Heung-Min, and Dejan Kulusevski, Spurs – surely – had enough talent on the pitch to show more life than they did. But after Milan finally roused themselves and spurned two clear chances late on, they were fortunate to still be in the tie.

The away fans, after sitting through 90 insipid minutes, had to wait another 45 minutes before being allowed to descend the tower slopes, and were then held again in an increasingly cramped space before being able to leave the stadium. Once more, they had to traverse the circuitous route to the metro station, which on arrival was overcrowded, with station staff seemingly unable to control the traffic. Some made it inside, only to be kicked off the train further down the line as the system shut down for the night. They emerged from stations not knowing where they were or how to get back to their hotels, and were often unable to use phones because batteries had run down and power packs had not been allowed into the stadium. Perhaps they could have got a tram, but information that they were available hadn't been communicated. Those that managed to flag down taxis were invariably fleeced. Others had to walk for hours. Just another typical night of following your team away in Europe!

The attendance of 74,320 generated receipts of €9.2 million. The average price of a ticket was €122, and Milan fans who were not season ticket holders paid €99 for their tickets; prices that invoked much adverse comment. Perhaps the Spurs board, whose own pricing policy in the group stage of the competition had been criticised, could permit themselves a wry smile after deciding not to charge the maximum they could for the return leg.

*

Back in London, with Conte remaining in Italy and with Cristian Stellini temporarily covering for his boss, the first of two home derbies saw West Ham for the late Sunday kick-off. After progress the previous season, West Ham had been treading water – only one win since October – but kept the home team at bay in a turgid encounter, at least until the 56th minute.

A breakthrough arrived from the unlikely combination of Ben Davies and Emerson Royal, who maintained the transformative form that was keeping Pedro Porro on the sidelines, with Royal coolly finishing after Davies' marauding run into the box. West Ham never really looked like responding and Son was able to notch his first league goal since early January, just four minutes after coming on as a substitute for Richarlison.

Son was having a poor season but was making a mark as a substitute, scoring four in two appearances after racking up only one in the previous 20 league starts. Had he reached the stage where he would be best suited arriving late to exploit tiring and stretched defences, or were the tactics not getting the best from the previous season's Golden Boot joint winner? The three points took Spurs, improbably, into the top four again and more than a few of the

198

departing home fans wondered whether Conte's absence was beneficial for the team's health as well as his own.

*

Had Conte been present for the next game, it might not have aided his recovery. Since his acrimonious departure from the club he took to the title, Chelsea have had the upper hand over Spurs, but having won only twice in their previous 14 games, were the odds in favour of the home team?

After a scoreless and stuttering first half, other than a Højbjerg shot that struck a post and a Raheem Sterling strike at the other end, the most notable incident was when Hakim Ziyech received a red card for raising his arm against Emerson Royal. Referee Stuart Attwell subsequently rescinded and downgraded the red to a yellow after viewing the pitchside monitor. The deadlock was broken just after the restart thanks to a sumptuous strike by Oliver Skipp – his first goal for the club. Spurs now had the force behind them and after Son again set out his super-sub credentials – coming on for Kulusevski and delivering the corner from which Kane made it 2-0, turning the ball in at the far post after a headed flick from Eric Dier – it was game, set and match. Two derby wins, four goals with no reply, and a tightening grip on a top-four place. Spurs were still not providing much entertainment, but if there was a plan, it was working.[36]

*

A successful trip to Sheffield in midweek for the fifth round of the FA Cup would continue the good run and firmly put the season back on track. The

---

[36] On February 23rd, the Government issued a White Paper on the governance of the game. The headlines were the introduction of an independent regulator to ensure tighter financial controls with transparency and accountability in order that clubs could survive and prosper. Further, no longer will owners be able to change the location of the club and its constituent elements – name, colours, logo – without consulting fans and obtaining regulatory approval. However, a redistribution of funds between the Premier League and the rest of professional football was left to the authorities to sort out. A missed opportunity. While the Premier League is prepared for greater largesse, it is not prepared to accede to the 25% which the EFL rejected as a shared deal in 1997 and now demands. Its argument that 80% of what the EFL normally receives goes to the Championship, whose clubs invariably spend more on wages than they earn despite their being some owners such as Bet365 who are wealthier than some Premier League clubs, is not without merit. Haggling will no doubt continue until the White Paper forms the basis of law.

Championship side was in contention for promotion, but Spurs surely had enough to get past them. With Arsenal, Chelsea, and Liverpool all having fallen by the wayside, the cup offered a real opportunity to secure the trophy that counted for so much with Spurs fans.

A year ago, at the same stage in the competition, Spurs had lamely conceded to Middlesbrough, another Championship side. Surely, they would not underestimate their opponents and do anything but field their strongest available team? Yet, that is exactly what they did. And out of the cup they went due to a late strike from the Sheffield substitute, Illiman Ndiaye. The victors added insult to injury by (probably) assuming that a Tottenham victory was a foregone conclusion, resting a number of first-team choices as they had a bigger prize in reach: promotion to the Premier League. The vapid display by the Premier League side was an insult to the 4,782 travelling fans, and a blot on the history of the club that had once, not so long ago, held the record for the most FA Cup wins.

Under Pochettino, Mourinho, and now Conte (though he was in Italy with Stellini on the touchline), Spurs had treated the domestic cups with disdain. Was there no one at the club who appreciated how vital a trophy, after 15 years without one, could be in building belief and confidence? Steve Perryman regularly refers to how important the 1981 success was in providing the impetus for the teams of the 1980s to attain five top-four finishes in the decade, plus win the FA Cup once more in 1982, and also the UEFA Cup in 1984. Did Conte and Stellini appreciate the significance of the tie? With reference to precedent, if Irving Scholar had been their boss, he surely would have told them, 'Of course, I'm not telling you who to pick, but I am letting you know just how important this competition is to our club'. If the current chairman conveyed this message, then it was studiously ignored.

*

A demoralised and increasingly angry support travelled back late from Sheffield on the Wednesday and set off for Wolverhampton on the Saturday, trying to look on the positive side, namely, that Spurs could now focus on the Champions League and the Premier League. But Spurs were once more underwhelming, and ended up on the wrong side of a 1-0 scoreline.

Team selection looked a mess. As Tim Spiers observed in *The Athletic*, 'Antonio Conte and Spurs have utterly failed to use their squad properly.' Kane, Romero and Kulesevski had been rested against Sheffield United supposedly because the Wolves fixture was more important. They returned, but the in-form Royal was left on the sidelines together with the UEFA-suspended Eric Dier, apparently with the Milan game in mind. Were Spurs ever going to play the game in front of them or constantly prepare for the next?

But what particularly caught Spiers's eye was the substitution made on the 77th minute when the score was 0-0. Needing a goal, Spurs did not send on the £60 million summer acquisition Richarlison, nor the January surprise swoop Arnaut Danjuma, but Lucas Moura, who they had been prepared to let leave as a free agent. 'Not to diminish Moura's abilities,' wrote Spiers, but 'to pick him ahead of Richarlison and Danjuma spoke volumes'. As, he said, did the timing of the substitution, coming after Wolves boss Julen Lopetegui had radically altered his tactics with five changes, two of whom combined for the winner. 'Lopetegui was proactive. Conte was reactive. Wolves improved. Spurs regressed,' was Spiers's verdict. He wasn't wrong.

Spurs had shuffled the unit that had delivered three wins and three clean sheets in four league games to literally pointless effect. A loss of impetus and two defeats was hardly the ideal preparation to face Milan in their attempt to overturn a 1-0 deficit to continue their European campaign.

*

On the 8th of March, London awoke to a thick blanket of snow and still-swirling flakes. It was the day of the decisive Champions League second leg round-of-16. By evening, the snow had cleared and freezing rain now doused the 61,602 who had navigated their way to the stadium via a transport system that invariably is unable to cope whenever there is a change in the weather.

Doug Bagley hosted his Milan friends, and accompanied the 1,600 members of the Curva Sud who marched up the High Road before the kick-off. Among them was Barone, now 73 years old, a legendary figure among the Milan Ultras, and Bagley was there to shake his hand as he arrived at Seven Sisters station.

As kick-off approached, the home crowd generated plenty of noise, the South Stand to the fore with flags and songs. They sensed a special effort was required. And Conte was back on the touchline.

Within 30 minutes, the enthusiasm had evaporated. Spurs were listless, while Milan were happy to let them be so, content in their 1-0 lead. The link between midfield and attack was sporadic, leaving Kane, Son and Kulusevski starved of service. When Milan did probe, the home defence looked jittery and disorganised and absolutely nothing of note was achieved.

Not a shot on target.

Not a moment of excitement.

The simple truth – that a goal was needed to force extra time and two for victory – didn't seem to have penetrated the players' minds, and the second half followed the same pattern as the first. Richarlison was brought on as Spurs belatedly realised what was at stake and the much-vaunted Pedro Porro replaced Ivan Perišić – one apparently vital piece in Conte's jigsaw replacing another. Then Romero rounded off a performance of imbecility with the second of two reckless yellow card tackles and was justifiably dismissed.

With his team down to 10 men in a knockout tie when it desperately needed a goal, Conte's response was perverse, and the withdrawal of Kulesevski in favour of Davinson Sánchez drew a chorus of boos from supporters who knew what was needed even if their manager didn't. In the dying minutes of added time, Kane got a header on target; the only clear chance created over 90 minutes. And that was that. A workmanlike Milan were through to the last eight of the world's foremost club competition courtesy of a solitary goal and Spurs' ineptitude. The failure to score over three hours was a damning indictment of Conte's joyless regime, but the manager himself seemed indifferent to the situation, telling the media after the game, 'My contract expires in June, we will see – they might sack me even before the end of the season, who knows, maybe they are disappointed.' Maybe.

The best that Spurs could now hope for was a top-four finish and the Champions League spot that went with it, but what is the point of qualifying if you are going to exit so meekly – which was the criticism thrown at Arsenal for so long – at the cost of millions of euros?

More pertinently, was a top-four finish really attainable from an outfit producing dour, predictable football week in week out; one that seemed reluctant to utilise the resources at its disposal? Since Spurs had challenged for the title and reached a Champions League final, Daniel Levy had made three managerial decisions which had brought the club to its current sorry state. Jack Pitt-Brooke observed in *The Athletic*, 'So long as he (Conte) stays in the dugout, it is hard to see Spurs playing with the confidence or freedom required to make the most of the obvious talent they have in their squad. Picturing the season ending in anything other than a miserable drift to fifth or sixth is difficult.'

During the game, a power cut closed the popular Shelf Bar. At the Goal Line Bar, Apple Pay machines stopped working. The high ticket prices were justified by the board as reflecting the superb facilities. But on the night, it seemed Spurs were no more able to deliver to their supporters off the pitch than on it. Perhaps a win provides a different perspective, and maybe the Milan fans were inured to poor facilities. 'You have a beautiful stadium. Milan need to build a new stadium and leave San Siro,' said one of them. 'And the New White Hart Lane would be a great role model. Modern, roomy and identifying. Congratulations.'

The sense now was not if but *when* Conte's contract would be brought to a premature end. Some fans had chanted Pochettino's name and his time in charge certainly chimed with the culture of the club and was the most successful of the ENIC era. Of course, other coaches – Luis Enrique, Thomas Tuchel, Oliver Glasner and Luciano Spalletti – were mentioned as possibilities but would any of them regard it as a privilege to manage Tottenham Hotspur and be able to work hand-in-glove with Levy?

After the firing of José Mourinho, Jürgen Klinsmann revealed that, not for the first time, he had thrown his hat into the ring only to feel that the board had an agenda that did not welcome any input from him; a telling illustration of the unwillingness of Levy and his colleagues to think outside the box or to acknowledge they might be barking up the wrong tree. Moreover, despite increasingly strident calls for them to go, they were going nowhere.

With 12 games now left to save the season, the biggest surprise would be if Conte was still on the touchline at Elland Road when Spurs visited Leeds for their 38th fixture.

14. SUPER MANAGER LAND

Not even the combination of a Saturday 3pm kick-off and the imminent approach of British summertime could put a spring in the step of many who made their way to the Tottenham Hotspur Stadium. All the same, over 61,000 still turned up on the 11th of March to see the team play Nottingham Forest – testament to the omnipotence of the Premier League and the powers of endurance of the home faithful (the barbed comments by Antonio Conte notwithstanding). In the press conference before the game, he admitted, 'The patience of the fans has finished. I feel this, the players feel this, this does not help the situation… I am putting everything in trying to build something. I understand that maybe it's not enough.' So, there you had it. The fans who wanted to be entertained, who wanted some success, who wanted to see some modicum of ambition and who paid a pretty penny for it, were 'not helping'.

Earlier in the week, in an interview for Brazilian TV, Richarlison had added fuel to the fire by describing the season bluntly as 's**t' and revealing his displeasure at his treatment. 'Yesterday, they asked me to take a test at the gym, that if I was good, I would go to the game and, at the time of the game, they left me on the bench. These are things that it is not possible to understand,' he said. Conte retorted that the striker was 'selfish' and he had 'apologised'. Nonetheless, he was selected alongside Son Heung-

Min and Harry Kane against Forest, replacing Dejan Kulusevski, who had fallen below his habitual high standard following the break for the World Cup. Ben Davies came in for Ivan Perišić and Pedro Porro for Emerson Royal.

A Kane header opened the scoring on 19 minutes, and he added a second from the penalty spot shortly afterwards. In doing so, he racked up another milestone, becoming only the third player in Premier League history to score 20 goals or more in six separate seasons – a feat previously accomplished only by Alan Shearer and Sergio Agüero.

Richarlison thought he had made his point by scoring after just three minutes, but the strike was ruled out. He did, though, set up Son for Spurs' third goal just past the hour for what appeared to be a routine victory. But, once again, the team eased up instead of driving home their superiority. Forest pulled a goal back, then were awarded a penalty deep into added time. It was saved by Fraser Forster, and a grateful Spurs maintained fourth place, six points ahead of Liverpool, who had surprisingly lost to Bournemouth in the early kick-off.

*

An unchanged line-up was named for the following Saturday's visit to bottom-of-the-table Southampton. Within the first 10 minutes, each team had lost a player to injury, with the unfortunate Richarlison replaced by Kulusevski and the home team replacing Armel Bella-Kotchap with Mohammed Salisu. As half-time approached, two more injuries and substitutions broke the flow, again one for each side – Perišić for Davies, and Ainsley Maitland-Niles for Jan Bednarek. The stoppages stymied any creativity but just before half-time Porro delivered the first real moment of quality by cutting in from the right wing and hammering a shot into the roof of the net for a half-time lead.

It was conceded almost immediately after the second half began, though, as Che Adams levelled after just 47 seconds. However, a Kane header – his ninth, to equal the record of the most headed goals in a season by Duncan Ferguson of Everton – and a fine strike from Perišić, his first goal for Spurs, looked to have secured the points. 'Conteball', however, entails that leads are to be defended, not built upon, and once again the opposition were invited to take control. Inevitably, Theo Walcott reduced the deficit on 76 minutes, and Conte's response was left to the last four minutes. He replaced Porro with Royal in a straight positional swap and withdrew Kulusevski for a defensive midfielder, Pape Matar Sarr, with unfortunate consequences. In added time, Matar Sarr was erroneously adjudged to have fouled Maitland-Niles and James Ward-Prowse scored the resultant penalty with the last kick of the match for a 3-3 draw.

For Spurs, it was definitely two points thrown away, and to a side staring relegation in the face, no less. Fans headed back to cars and coaches – a train strike making one of the most accessible away trips trickier than usual – shaking their heads and wondering how this team could possibly still be in fourth place. Then, shortly after 6pm, Conte detonated.

The post-match press conference was described by seasoned journalists as one of the most extraordinary they had ever witnessed. It began innocuously enough with a question about the controversial late penalty decision. Conte answered, 'If we are going to discuss about the penalty it means we don't want to see other situations. For the penalty, for me, it was not a penalty. I stop, we close the situation. The worst situation is what was happening on the pitch. What has been happening in the last few months, what's happening in this, my second season.'

He was visibly agitated.

And gathering momentum.

'I think it's much better to go into the problem, because the problem is that for another time, we showed that we are not a team. We are 11 players that go onto the pitch. I see selfish players. I see players that don't want to help each other and don't put their heart [into it]. If I have to compare last season and this season, I said to improve, now we are worse in this aspect. When you are not a team, everything can happen, in any moment. But here, we're used to it for a long time. The club has the responsibility for the transfer market, every coach that stayed here has the responsibility.

'And the players? The players? Where are the players? I can tell you that if you want to be competitive, if you want to fight, you have to improve this aspect. And now this aspect, for me, in this moment is really, really low. And I see only 11 players that play for themselves. They are used to it here. They don't play for something important. They don't want to play under pressure, they don't want to play under stress. It is easy in this way.'

The previous week, it had been the fans' fault.

Now it was the players who were the guilty party.

Conte then moved on to criticise the owner and the culture of the club. 'Tottenham's story is this. Twenty years there is the owner and they never won something, but why? The fault is only for the club, or for every manager that stay here? And now, until now I try to hide the situation but now, no, because I repeat I don't want to see what I have seen today because this is unacceptable, also for the respect for the fans. They follow us, pay [for] the tickets and to see the team another time to have this type of performance, for me, I repeat, this is unacceptable. We have to think a lot, we have to think a lot about this. Not only the club, not only the manager, the staff. The players have to be involved in this situation because it is time to change this situation if Tottenham want to change. If they want to continue in this way, they can change manager, a lot of managers, but the situation cannot change. Believe me.' Conte paused, then abruptly added, 'Thank you very much', and walked out.

Here was a man who had given up on his players (an atypical situation of the dressing room losing the manager), his employers, and his job. Seemingly, it was everybody's fault but his own. In a 10-minute diatribe of discontent and indignation, he had destroyed his relationship with the club.

Nevertheless, there was more than an element of truth in what he had said; telling home truths is a tactic usually deployed to improve the existing situation. Conte's condemnation fuelled a damaging trope. 'Lads, it's Tottenham,' was the phrase infamously used by Sir Alex Ferguson, the implication being that the club was institutionally incapable of winning when it mattered. Arsenal fans deploy a blunter version on the frequent occasions when their neighbours fail to 'turn up' at their ground – 'Tottenham Hotspur, you'll always be s**t'. And now here was Spurs' own manager making the same unfavourable assessment.

On the coaches carrying Spurs fans home from Southampton, there was widespread anger as news of Conte's extraordinary outburst filtered through. But there were also those who shared his opinion of the players' performances, and who quickly picked up on his reference to 'the owner'. So much at Spurs was seen through the prism of predetermined positions, and some fans were eager to seize on anything that could be used to validate their views. For the majority, though, the stinging condemnation of a fundamental facet of their very existence was deeply wounding.

As broadcaster and long-time Spurs fan Danny Kelly said, 'I don't take kindly to people torching the things I love… Antonio Conte didn't actually say anything that was untrue. The criticisms are valid. Whether it was a wise move for a manager to say that in public is another thing…

'There's a phrase about telling the truth, the whole truth, and nothing but the truth, and what Antonio did was to tell some of the truth. But a good part of what he said was made meaningless by the fact that he didn't address his own role. That's because he's part of a new super-elite of managers who see themselves not as managing clubs day to day, but as having a career path in which to be successful as they move from club to club to club.

'Coaches like Bill Nicholson, Brian Clough, Bill Shankly, Alex Ferguson, they coached clubs for a decade or more, and they were happy to do that. The new super-elite of managers are not, and they are forever managing their CV in public. They are never responsible for anything and they are always like beaten generals – one tank battalion short of victory.'

Not wanting your club to be publicly trashed, not wanting your manager to give opponents material to hammer you with for years to come, that's not avoiding home truths or sucking up to the board. That's being a committed, loyal fan. In his exasperation, Conte demonstrated his ignorance of the institution that employed him, one that had existed since 1882. Won nothing for 20 years? There's the small, but not insignificant, matter of the League Cup in 2008. The 'empty trophy cabinet' badinage also disregarded the fact that Tottenham Hotspur was the first to accomplish the modern Double, the first British team to capture a European trophy, the club that once held the record for the most FA Cup wins, and carried off at least one trophy in every decade from 1950 to 2010.

Manchester United don't discount the Busby Babes or the triumvirate of Law, Charlton, and Best because it's history. Arsenal don't discount the accomplishments of Herbert Chapman because they occurred nearly a century ago. Successful clubs tap into their past to help shape their future. (Unless they can just buy it, which Spurs can't and won't do.) Heritage, tradition and identity are integral parts of the brand which is created in the hearts and minds of supporters. And the most powerful brands are football clubs because they are limited only by their partisanship, the extent of their fan base. There are local brands such as Accrington Stanley, national brands such as Stoke City, and international brands of which Tottenham Hotspur Football Club is among a select few with millions of followers worldwide.

Carling may be your lager of choice, but that doesn't preclude taking advantage of a special Heineken offer and there is no guilt attached to the short-term promiscuous purchase. But of the thousands who have had to put up with the dross served up this season in N17, in all likelihood not a single one of them contemplated nipping down the road to N5, where more entertainment and better value for money was almost certainly to be found.

Conte had been backed more than any manager before him by Daniel Levy but he still apparently could not work with the tools he had been given. Tellingly, good players had regressed on his watch, and his tactics not only failed to optimise the squad's strengths, they exacerbated its weaknesses. It was Conte's job to get the best out of the resources he had been given, not to make excuses about why he couldn't. And you don't get the best out of people by telling them they are not up to scratch. The manager who had questioned the existence of a winning mentality waited 150 minutes into a 180-minute Champions League knockout tie before going on the offensive, and then proceeded to swap a forward for a defender when a goal was needed. The manager who questioned his players' commitment dropped key personnel for an eminently winnable FA Cup fixture[37] that offered a clearer route to the final stages than it had for many years, but one which he considered to be insignificant.

It must be remembered that Conte had endured a traumatic few months. The loss of three close friends and a serious operation had to be reconciled with the day-to-day demands of a highly intensive job played out in the media spotlight. Only someone with a heart of stone could fail to empathise with what he had endured. In the final analysis, a supposedly elite manager on an eight-figure salary – who kept reminding everyone he is a serial winner – has to be held responsible for the failure to achieve the objectives for which he was hired.

The simple truth may be that Conte doesn't possess a winning mentality. He has, or had, a

---

[37] The Cup Final used to be the highlight of the season. But the FA devalued their crown jewel by allowing the holders Manchester United to withdraw in favour of participation in the Club World Championship in 2000, in the forlorn hope of boosting their ultimately futile bid for the 2006 World Cup. Piling mistake upon mistake, they succumbed to Premier League pressure and dropped replays after the fourth round, and opted to use Wembley for the semi-finals. But it was still the second most important domestic trophy and one that attracted a large worldwide television audience.

winning method whose timespan is finite. It may yet prove successful again in his homeland, but at the very top level, football is a constantly evolving business. Staying resolutely with your trusted and tested formula will eventually reveal itself to be outmoded and leave you wanting and out of touch – as Arsène Wenger and José Mourinho have discovered. To have a winning mentality is to move with the times, to absorb innovations and to face changing conditions by constantly refreshing your methods, your way of working. Changing your staff, an open mindset, and accepting new challenges are the reasons why Sir Alex Ferguson and Pep Guardiola have, over decades, won countless trophies under different circumstances. They are the rare exceptions that demonstrate a winning mentality that few others – and certainly not Conte – possess.

'I think Daniel Levy knows,' said Kelly, 'that Spurs fans, particularly ones of a certain age, will settle for seeing good football and the team having a good chance of winning a trophy. They would rather risk losing 3-2 by trying to win 3-2. But we have this dichotomy whereby he proceeds to appoint three defensive coaches, one after the other, two of whom were superstars in that self-appointed firmament of elite managers… What they have done has run contrary to the grain at Spurs and those managers don't have the best interests of the club at heart. I also think Levy has been starstruck by the likes of Mourinho and Conte.'

Charlie Eccleshare wrote in *The Athletic*, 'Failing to forecast that Conte's best days might have been behind him – as Mourinho's proved to be when he pitched up at Spurs – is one of the charges levelled against Levy. Was another Chelsea hand-me-down, known for reactive football, really what was required less than seven months after ditching one matching that description? Especially given he (Levy) had spoken about the need for a head coach with 'Spurs DNA' in the intervening period.' There were legitimate and pressing questions to be asked of the board – £215 million of talent out on loan was just one clear indication of the lack of direction and cohesion – and the problems highlighted were not being acknowledged.

With a break in the Premier League season to make way for the qualifying rounds of Euro 2024, the spotlight dimmed on the domestic agenda, but the silence from Spurs was deafening and Conte remained in his post. Then, after eight days, late on the evening of Sunday the 27th of March, the announcement came that Conte had left 'by mutual agreement'. A brief statement revealed that Cristian Stellini, Conte's assistant, would take over for the remainder of the season, and concluded with Levy saying, 'We have 10 Premier League games remaining and we have a fight on our hands for a Champions League place. We all need to pull together. Everyone has to step up to ensure the highest possible finish for our club and amazing, loyal supporters.'

Of all the names thought to be on the club's wish list, Stellini was conspicuous by his absence. This was a case of 'if it's broke, don't fix it'. Just continue down the wrong road with a different, more inexperienced driver, and totally ignore the probable new manager impetus that the appointment of a club hero such as Mauricio Pochettino or Jürgen Klinsmann would undoubtedly have provided.

The plea to 'pull together' further irritated fans whose patience with Levy and the board was running out, and the frustration was exemplified by the fact there was no alternative in sight. There was talk of tension between Joe Lewis's daughter, Vivienne, who was an increasingly visible presence at games, and the executive trio of Levy, Donna-Maria Cullen, and Matthew Collecott. However, there seemed little prospect of internal change in the absence of any realistic bid for the club.

A small but vociferous hardcore of Levy/ENIC 'outers' – whose aim appeared to be to make things as unpleasant as possible in order to bring about change – were strident in their denunciations of anyone who didn't agree with them. Yet some looked beyond their bluster and found some common ground. As Winter wrote, the Spurs board 'has the power, but not the authority' and he added witheringly that 'many good, conscientious people' who worked at the club 'deserve better leadership'. He asked, 'Who can stand up to be counted at Spurs, a great club with a loyal staff and a huge, passionate, frustrated fanbase?', adding that 'Conte's important critique of daring dreamily rather than doing determinedly was lost amidst the smoke of his explosive farewell press conference at St Mary's Stadium. If Levy is as shrewd as his CV suggests, however, he will heed Conte's counsel, however corrosive.'

And Winter added that he thought it 'a stain and a shame' on the role Levy had played that it was the Tottenham Hotspur Supporters' Trust that had provided 'the most thoughtful observations' on Conte's departure, not the person who had appointed and worked with him.

As if to prove Winter's point, the club's next move brought to mind a comment from a previous crisis. 'Who knew it was possible to shoot yourself in more feet than you were born with?'

Two days after Conte's departure, Managing Director of Football Fabio Paratici rolled out platitudes about how the decision to jettison the manager had been the right one, and now everyone needed to stick together. Paratici's video – which looked to be a rather unprofessional DIY effort rather than the sort of authoritative communication to be expected from a major club – was released late on the evening of Tuesday the 28th of March. On the morning of Wednesday the 29th of March, FIFA announced that Paratici was to be banned from all football activities worldwide for two years.

Concerns had already been raised regarding his role after he received a 30-month ban from the Italian football authorities following investigations of financial irregularities at Juventus, his previous club. It was widely believed that a FIFA ban was a possibility and, therefore, it beggared belief that no one had contacted FIFA before putting Paratici up as the company spokesperson at such a crucial moment. True to form, the club were quick to point out that they were the real victims. Less than 24 hours after the FIFA announcement, an indignant statement claimed, 'This (FIFA) committee deliberation has been taken with no advance notice to any of the parties involved. We are urgently seeking further clarification'. Once again, anything negative could be laid at someone else's door.

*

With 10 games remaining, the club was in turmoil. There was no evidence of forward-thinking, with the result that it was led by a disciple and former assistant of the man they had just fired. Would it suddenly emerge that Conte's number two really harboured ambitions to use properly the attacking talents at his disposal, or – more likely – would it mean more of the same underwhelming football? The move only made sense in the context of Spurs being unable to attract a top-rank first-team coach.

Nevertheless, a top-four finish was still a possibility, albeit an increasingly remote one. But even if qualification for the Champions League was somehow achieved, what would be the point if this season's campaign set any precedent? And, if it was not to be, would the Europa League or Europa Conference League be the highlight of next season? Or, in the worst case (and one that hadn't been experienced for some time), what would be the implication of drifting back into mid-table mediocrity? For once, the cliché of 'taking each game as it comes' was particularly apt.

15. WHO'S FOOLING WHO?

April began, as always, on All Fools Day, an occurrence that would prove particularly apt and prescient for Spurs supporters two days later.

Errors were much in evidence when Spurs resumed action at Goodison Park on Sky Monday Night Football against an Everton side benefiting from some new manager positivity after Sean Dyche replaced Frank Lampard. Nonetheless, the threat of relegation loomed over the home side, which had never been out of the Premier League, and a malaise had developed over the season, prompting a protest march before the game. Inside the ground, the fractious atmosphere was compounded by chants of 'Levy out' from the away section. Two clubs at opposite ends of the table in the world's most affluent league; two instances of a disconnect with fans and a mistrust of leadership.

The game began much as expected between two sides in a poor vein of form, with few notable incidents to allay the fears of either sets of supporters. Then, just past the hour, Harry Kane and Abdoulaye Doucouré clashed on the touchline in front of the dugout, and the Everton man reacted by putting a hand in his opponent's face. The referee was left with no option but to bring out the red card.

The Everton bench, and the home crowd, however, were incensed by Kane's theatrics, and cries of 'cheat' reverberated around the ground. Certainly, Kane had exaggerated the contact, but when others have reacted in a similar manner it has often been excused as clever gamesmanship. Spurs fans also recalled when the boot was on the other foot in the infamous 'Battle of the Bridge' against Chelsea in May 2016 when Mousa Dembélé had clawed at Diego Costa's face and rightfully received a six-game ban for his misdemeanour.

Kane's unpopularity grew further when he was awarded a penalty minutes later, converting it to send the visitors temporarily back into fourth place and Everton to the brink of the drop. Spurs were now leading against 10 men short on confidence in front of an increasingly agitated and volatile crowd. The obvious tactic was to press home their advantage, but Cristian Stellini's response was infuriatingly passive. He instructed the team to drop back, to preserve the lead, thereby inviting pressure from a desperate opponent. Everton took their cue. Spurs even contrived to lose their man advantage when Lucas Moura, brought on in the 82nd minute, was dismissed for a reckless tackle six minutes later. *The Guardian's* in-game commentator wrote, 'Spurs have the lead but seem desperate to give it away with some of the thickest passing in their own box you will ever see'.

On the 90th minute, the inevitable transpired when central defender Michael Keane, capitalising on the space left in front of the Spurs penalty area, moved forward unopposed and despatched a splendid strike into the roof of the net. Two vital points lost after one of Spurs' most witless performances for many a year – a simple case of refusing to learn from mistakes and paying the price.

*

The Everton game set nerves jangling five days later for the visit of Brighton & Hove Albion, a club with all of the desirable credentials that the Tottenham of 2023 lacked; a well-run, harmonious organisation with a clear vision and long-term perspective. What's more, Albion threatened to usurp Spurs' potential European place.[38]

Roberto De Zerbi, the Brighton manager, had taken offence at a perceived slight from Stellini in the Italian press[39] before the game, and the pre-match handshake became a pre-match altercation that set the tone for feisty exchanges between the two men throughout the afternoon. Brighton started on the front foot, but it was Son who broke the deadlock with a long-range shot for his 100th Premier League

----

[38] The 2021/22 Europa Conference League winners, Roma, earned €19.63 million whilst the Champions League winners, Real Madrid, received €133.7 million.

[39] A headline in *La Gazetta dello Sport,* had read: "De Zerbi exploited all of Graham Potter's work at Brighton."

goal, making him the first Asian player to achieve the milestone. Lewis Dunk soon took advantage of lax marking – what had the three consecutive defensively-minded managers been coaching exactly? – to deservedly equalise. Every marginal decision had gone in Spurs' favour, so much so that the Professional Game Match Officials Ltd (PGMOL) felt compelled to apologise later to Brighton for the errors made by the referee, Stuart Attwell, and VAR for not awarding a penalty for Pierre-Emile Højbjerg's challenge on Kaoru Mitoma.

After the touchline fracas intensified, resulting in both managers being sent off, Spurs stirred themselves and Kane struck a late winner, his 76th match-winning goal for the club. It was yet another landmark that underlined his vital contribution over the years – and the desperate straits the team would have been in this season without him.

*

The following weekend against Bournemouth, Son, again, gave the home side the lead and he and his teammates seemed, at last, to click into gear. However, a well-organised opponent refused to fold, and characteristically poor defending led to first Matias Vina's equaliser and then, as the second half got underway, Dominic Solanke putting the visitors in front.

The 'Levy out' chants grew more vociferous and Davinson Sánchez was shamefully jeered as he entered for the injured Clément Lenglet, then sarcastically applauded when he was replaced after just 22 minutes on the pitch. As *The Guardian's* John Brewin observed, 'A game that might have been out of sight had lurched into a trademark Tottenham existential crisis'.

With two minutes to go, Arnaut Danjuma looked as though he had salvaged a point, but then Dango Ouattara surged past an immobile midfield and slammed home a 95th-minute winner. A case of what goes around comes around – Spurs having pulled a similar last-minute iron from the fire in the October encounter on the south coast.

The decision to retain Antonio Conte's setup whilst jettisoning Conte himself looked increasingly inexplicable, while the possibility of tumbling down the table was disturbingly realistic, especially with the imminent prospect of having to face three in-form rivals – Newcastle United, Manchester United and Liverpool – for a now unlikely top-four finish.

As fans digested the latest setback, news emerged of a rare public appearance some weeks before (on March 14th) by Daniel Levy at the Cambridge Union. (What more appropriate choice of location when criticised for having an aloof and disdainful attitude towards supporters than one of the UK's elite universities?[40])

Levy spoke of his support for the club since the age of eight, and his journey from being a comprehensive school kid who was told he'd never make anything of himself to a job in investment banking via Cambridge. He made no bones about having entered football as a business decision, saying, 'It was purely an investment opportunity.' He later said that he was 'a fan first and an investor second'.

Asked about the rationale behind the new stadium, Levy said part of the reason was that, 'We couldn't get the young kids into games because there were no tickets available'. Had a journalist been present, they would have been justified in asking how this noble aspiration squared with charging some of the highest ticket prices in Europe. But the question was not asked.

Levy claimed that the club had 'progressed enormously' in the 22 years since he had taken over, adding that, 'When we first came to Tottenham, winning was making sure we stayed in the Premier League'. Andy Dunn, the Chief Sportswriter at *The*

---

[40] The event was also staged to provide Levy the opportunity to meet with graduates of his club's sponsored school who had been accepted at Cambridge – underlining the kind of commitment to education that goes largely unrecognised in football.

Mirror, applied some journalistic rigor to the answers. 'There is a brand-new shiny stadium, for sure,' he observed, 'and their average finishing position in the league during his 22-year reign is about 6.1 compared to about 8.8 in the equivalent period of time that preceded his arrival. But during that time, Spurs won three FA Cups, one League Cup, and a UEFA Cup compared to the one League Cup won in the Levy era.' (Spurs had) 'finished this number of places above the drop zone respectively - 12, 5, 13, 10, 8, 4, 7, 8'. Dunn concluded that this was 'not earth-shatteringly good but hardly a consistent flirtation with disaster as Levy implies'.

Characteristically, Levy emphasised his responsibility to '30,000 shareholders ... most of them are fans who own the shares'. Those shareholders had 14.4% of Tottenham Hotspur Limited (THL), reduced to 12.5% by the equity raised in May 2022 that had been presented as a cash injection of £150m. There was little chance of it being increased as the club has steadfastly refused to consider proposals permitting fans to acquire a greater stake. It's a line Levy has frequently used, and it disingenuously presents the incumbent board as custodians of an army of small shareholders.[41]

---

[41] THL, which controls Tottenham Hotspur Football and Athletic Co Limited and Tottenham Hotspur Stadium Limited, is owned by ENIC Sports Inc,

For the majority of small shareholders – whose single share certificates often reside in a frame in the smallest room in the house – the implications are academic. In all likelihood, those shares are owned for reasons of sentiment rather than as an investment. And the suggestion that any decisions on investment or ownership are taken with any serious consideration given to the interests of minority shareholders is open to doubt.

Reverting to football matters, at one point, Levy was asked, 'You've been described as more painful to deal with than a hip replacement. How would you describe your negotiating style?' He replied, 'Firstly, that comment was from Alex Ferguson, who remains a friend. All I was doing was protecting the interests of my club. It shouldn't be seen as a negative.' Quite so. For all his faults, driving a hard bargain on behalf of his club should not be seen as one of them, and the fact that Ferguson's partisan criticism had become established as fair comment said more about the former Manchester United manager's ability to set the agenda than anything else.

Inevitably, Levy was asked about the chances of holding on to Kane if the club failed to secure a

---

which possesses 88.5% of the shares in THL and is, in turn, 100% owned by ENIC International Limited, whose shares are owned 70.6% by Lewis Family Trusts and 29.4% by Daniel Levy.

trophy. 'He can absolutely win a trophy at Spurs', Levy replied. 'But, you know, being a legend is also important. The fact that he's the top scorer for Tottenham Hotspur, he's making history. I hope one day there is a statue of Harry Kane outside our stadium.' A populist response that avoided answering the question. But a statue? The club had previously swatted away the claims of club legends to be recognised on the grounds that such legacy iconography did not fit 'the aesthetic' of the shiny new sports and entertainment dome. And yet now, apparently, there could be one of Kane, presumably if he didn't leave after his contract expires in 2024.

Dunn described Levy's performance as 'steadfastly delusional', adding that 'he speaks as though talking to a congregation who know very little about football or are in primary school'. For *Football London*, Spurs correspondent Alasdair Gold said, 'The session was an exercise for Levy in pointing the finger of blame at everyone for anything that has gone wrong at the club, including results, transfers and managerial hiring and firing, while talking up any achievement he could off the pitch from his two decades at the helm.'

*

Back on the pitch, Spurs entered a potentially defining week. It began with a visit to Newcastle on the 23rd of April, billed as the battle for the fourth Champions League spot. Despite their newfound wealth, Newcastle's rise from the depths – they sat third in the table – could not be accurately described as having been entirely bought. Eddie Howe, a likeable man with a decent track record but not the kind of 'big name' Spurs had allowed themselves to be seduced by, had built an effective and entertaining unit.

With St James' Park in full voice, Newcastle stormed into attack and Spurs, having reverted to a back four, were cut apart and a goal down within two minutes. Then it was two, and within nine minutes, the home side were 3-0 up. After 21 minutes, Spurs were 5-0 down; the worst start by any team in Premier League history. From the outset, they showed no desire, no urgency, no leadership – justifying Antonio Conte's scathing criticism that they are 'selfish' and 'don't want to help each other'.

Hugo Lloris did not emerge for the second half, with the official explanation that he was injured. Kane pulled a goal back, singlehandedly working his opportunity and prompting a half-hearted chant of 'We're going to win 6-5' from the away support, high up behind the goal. But on 67 minutes, Callum Wilson added a sixth, his first touch after coming on as a substitute, an event the entire Spurs team seemed not to have noticed, such was his freedom to score.

This was humiliation, plain and simple. The embarrassment was such that the club reimbursed the travelling fans' ticket costs. Six points separated the two clubs, and Champions League football looked an implausible target for Spurs.

*

After 'Sunday bloody Sunday', it still took until the Tuesday for Levy to realise he had no choice but to sack Stellini and break with the Conte regime. He did what he could have done in the first place and appointed Ryan Mason until the end of the season. There is no doubting Mason's commitment, and following his enforced retirement as a player, he has more coaching experience than most 31-year-olds. Any hopes, however, centred more on his ability to restore some unity and passion than on him masterminding a home win – just three days after the Newcastle debacle – against a Manchester United side that manager Erik ten Hag seemed to have clicked into gear and into pole position for the final Champions League spot.

The pessimism seemed justified as United, through Jadon Sancho and Marcus Rashford, took a two-goal lead – prompting Spurs' Executive Director Donna-Maria Cullen to be caught on camera appearing to exclaim: 'It's s**t'. The television clip rapidly went viral on social media, invariably accompanied by a comment along the lines of 'Yes, it is, and whose fault is that?'

Perhaps it was a case of enough is enough, the nadir having been reached, or maybe Mason shamed them into a reaction. Whatever it was, Spurs came out for the second half and took the game to their opponents. The crowd sensed the change and responded. The 'Levy Out' chants and the boos were replaced by cries of 'Come on you Spurs.' Pedro Porro, with his first home goal for Spurs, reduced the arrears with a well-struck shot, and after both sides had scorned the easiest of chances through Bruno Fernandes and Eric Dier, respectively, Kane set up Son for the equaliser with 11 minutes to go. For the first time in weeks, both players and supporters left the stadium in good spirits, though conscious that another daunting task awaited them in three days' time.

*

Plus ça change, plus c'est la même chose.

At Anfield on the Sunday, the defence was ripped apart again by two goals in the first five minutes, and a unwise tackle by Cristian Romero gave away the penalty that led to the third with just a quarter of an hour on the clock. On Sky, Gary Neville joked that the ticket refunds should be put on direct debit. The time when the fans could be blamed for not getting behind the team had long gone; too many now utterly disgusted by the embarrassment attached to a once-proud shirt.

But Liverpool had been experiencing troubles of their own, and as the half wore on, Spurs burst into life, so much so that they could have been level by half time instead of just one down (once again through Kane). During the break, in a comic twist, a plane flew over the stadium dragging a banner that called for Liverpool's owners to go.

Mason demonstrated he understood the Tottenham Hotspur DNA. He urged his men forward and made positive, though belated, substitutions. On 77 minutes, Son scored and then, in the frenetic third minute of added time, former Everton star Richarlison brought the scores level with his first league goal of the season. Spurs had dredged up some of the old spirit, character, and belief, and had dug a point out in the most trying of circumstances.

But this was Spurs.

Their joy was short-lived. From the restart, Diogo Jota, who perhaps should not have remained on the pitch after a dreadful tackle on Oliver Skipp (maybe the PGMOL should write a nice, apologetic letter to Tottenham) pounced on an errant pass from Lucas Moura, who was a 90th minute – unnecessary – substitute for Porro. Jota ran unopposed into the box and scored the winner to make the result 4-3. *The Times's* headline – 'Match that redefined the term 'Spursy'' – summed up the afternoon.

Rarely has there been such a sense of deflation. It was the life of a Spurs fan encapsulated in one minute: pure joy to pure sorrow. What's next?

As Liverpool replaced Spurs in fifth position in the table and with the remaining fixtures against Crystal Palace, Aston Villa (who were also on 54 points), Brentford, and a final day visit to Leeds United, a slide down the table and out of Europe altogether appeared the most probable outcome.

16. IT ALL ENDS HERE

On the day of King Charles III's coronation, Spurs had a visit from the Palace.[42] The eyes of the world were on London and handling the crowds and guaranteeing the safety of the hundreds of dignitaries and the thousands of hoi polloi attending the ceremonies ensured that the security services had their work cut out. Most of the Premier League schedule had been moved, leaving just five fixtures on the day itself, with a game in N17 the only one in *any division* to go ahead in London.

Spurs' insistence on playing had apparently irked the police and authorities, and the surprise was that the Premier League had scheduled any games on Coronation Day at all. Just how such decisions are made and who is ultimately responsible for them can be *terra incognita* in which avoiding responsibility and passing the buck has been developed into a fine art. What can be deduced, though, is that the police may be able prevent London derbies kicking off after 4.45pm on a weekend but can't stop a club from playing when there's a Coronation.

---

[42] Which brings to mind a *Guardian* match report headline from 1970, 'Queen in brawl at Palace'. Crystal Palace had a Scottish forward called Gerry Queen.

Perhaps distracted by events at Westminster, perhaps numbed by the *septimana horribilis* the team had just endured, there was a muted atmosphere emanating from what was nonetheless a healthy crowd. An uninspiring afternoon concluded with Spurs winning after an indifferent performance against an underwhelming opponent. But even on a mundane day, Harry Kane sets records! His winning goal just before half time set a new Premier League mark for most headed goals in a season, his 10 eclipsing the previous nine by Duncan Ferguson of Everton. It was also his 209th Premier League goal, moving him up to second in the all-time charts behind Alan Shearer's 260.

*

Unfortunately, the following Saturday, normal service resumed with a bang at Villa Park, with Spurs one down after eight minutes. This was in a game against one of their rivals for a place in the Europa League or Europa Conference League – the Champions League was definitely out of reach. Villa were a revelation, moving up the table in an attractive and effective style, manager Unai Emery enjoying a new lease of life in England. When he took over on the 1st of November, Villa were facing relegation. Now, a European place beckoned. Douglas Luiz added Villa's second on 72 minutes and only a disputed last-minute penalty from Kane brought the travelling fans anything close to a cheer.

Spurs stayed above Villa in the table, albeit only on goal difference.

So many questions, so many problems. What progress had been made in the search for a new manager? Would anyone take the job without knowing who his Director of Football would be? And, did it make sense to recruit for each position separately? One name being touted by the media for the managerial role was Julian Nagelsmann, who had suddenly become available after Bayern Munich had surprisingly sacked him a few weeks earlier. He espoused a positive approach that Spurs fans were desperate to see again and the prospect of him taking over had generated some optimism. But the day before the Villa game Spurs had 'let it be known' they had 'ended their interest' in the highly rated candidate.

There was no official announcement, of course, which made the club look pretentious, as the withering response of Oliver Holt, the Chief Sportswriter of the *Daily Mail*, illustrated. 'Last week, Spurs let it be known that they had 'ended their interest' in appointing Julian Nagelsmann as their new manager,' he wrote. 'On the very same day, by pure coincidence, I ended my interest in opening the batting for England in the First Test against Australia at Edgbaston next month.' He called the mixture of 'face-saving fantasy and haughtiness' at a club he described as 'heading south fast' as being 'bitterly amusing'. And whoever saw fit to 'let it be known' had done so the day before a key game, which interim manager Ryan Mason and his players no doubt greatly appreciated.

A quick response from Spurs to take issue with Holt would have come as no surprise. The club had gained a reputation for stern rebukes over media coverage it did not approve of; a self-defeating approach that made it more difficult to generate positive PR.

In Daniel Levy's traditional end of season message to fans, after his rather awkward and unconvincing sign-off of 'COYS, Daniel' when he announced the sacking of Cristian Stellini, he sensibly reverted to a more formal approach. Levy stated that it had been 'an immensely difficult season' and 'we made footballing decisions over recent seasons based on ambition and a desire to bring success to our Club and they have not delivered what we had hoped.' As a result of all this, a 'thorough and rigorous review of our footballing operations' was underway. There was no recognition of whether, just perhaps, any mistakes at the highest level may have been made and needed to be learned from.

Spurs blogger Alan Fisher was right on the money in his response. 'Any football club depends on three elements, a manager/coach, recruitment and finance,' he said. 'Seldom in the 22 years he's been in charge has Daniel Levy successfully aligned all three, and when he has, those fleeting moments now seem like outliers… The underlying fundamental problems have become ingrained in the club's fabric, which is motheaten and rotting away. There's no plan, and there's no plan because the board still do not know what they want this club to be. They want success but do not know how to create and sustain it. They do not understand how to pick the right coach or how to support their chosen man.'

*

Meanwhile, there were two final acts in store, the first being the last game of the season at the Tottenham Hotspur stadium against Brentford who, like previous visitors Brighton, were a well-run club with a clear vision of who they are and how to go about their business, and merited their current position knocking on the door of the leading pack.

Spurs started atypically, with an early goal after eight minutes. It was a beauty scored, of course, by Kane who seized on a short back-heeled free kick from Kulusevski and unleashed a curling 25-yarder into the top corner. It was a breathtaking strike that brought a rare moment of delight to those watching. That made it 28 Premier League goals now and counting. Spurs actually looked like a unit and created chances, reflecting the attacking approach that Ryan Mason wanted. But they were not converting them and, as expected, there were consequences. Half-time came, and Brentford manager Thomas Frank changed his team's approach so thoroughly that his side wrestled the initiative from Spurs. The result was a forgone conclusion well before Yoane Wissa, making light of Ivan Toney's absence,[43] had scored Brentford's third.

At the conclusion of the final home game, fans are encouraged to stay behind to show their appreciation. However, by the time the players had returned to the pitch, there were barely a few thousand remaining from the 61,514 who bore witness to yet another low point to add to the substantial 2022/2023 collection.

*

And, so to Leeds, for the denouement.

The last time Spurs were at Elland Road they had beaten Leeds so convincingly that it was the final act in Marcelo Bielsa's tenure. Since then, the Leeds board had blundered from one managerial appointment to the next; Jesse Marsch, Javi Gracia, and now Sam Allardyce who had been given a mere four games to safeguard their Premier League place

---

[43] The Brentford talisman and leading goalscorer with 20 goals had been banned from all football for eight months and fined £50,000 by the FA after being found guilty of 232 breaches of the betting rules. Players are simply not allowed to bet or provide betting information. Toney admitted the offences, showed remorse, and his club, in turn, continued to support him.

before arriving at a point where even a victory would not be enough to save them if Everton won.

Two minutes in, Kane scored the easiest of goals. When the cheers of the away fans died down, it was their 'Levy Out' chants, rather than those directed at the Leeds board, that were distinctly audible. The vast majority of the 3,000 in the away end were joining in, taking the chance to vent their frustration.

Leeds were hapless. 'No fight, no unity, no hope', as the headline writers put it. So, it was a surprise when the score remained 1-0 at half time. However, just after the restart, Pedro Porro made it two and Leeds' fate looked sealed. All the same, Jack Harrison pulled one back but no sooner than he had done so than Kane added a third, and the home fans began to chant 'sack the board'. The away section joined in, and soon the entire ground was singing in unison. Football really can bring people together.

In a more positive frame of mind, Spurs supporters were also celebrating Arsenal's failure to win the title, Manchester City having been crowned champions the previous week. A small cynical ray of sunshine in the season's gloom, to be able to glorify in their neighbour's disappointment. 'We're all having a party, when Arsenal f**k it up' chorused the Spurs support. That prompted a debate between two of them over whether the chant should be 'cos Arsenal f****d it up' because it had already happened. Possibly the first time an argument about grammar and tense has been pursued in such circumstances.

Everton were winning and clearly Leeds could not now do anything to help themselves. One of their fans ran onto the pitch and evaded stewards before being wrestled to the ground. It took about a half a dozen of them to subdue him and haul him off. 'He's got more fight than you' chorused the home fans to their players.

In injury time, Lucas Moura came on for his swansong in a Spurs shirt. Almost immediately he was passed the ball on the right flank, turned inwards, and headed straight for goal. His mazy run left Leeds defenders trailing in his wake before he slammed home his side's fourth goal. It was a fine effort, despite the paucity of opposition. Lucas looked overwhelmed as his teammates and the entire bench engulfed him, then raised him above their heads in front of the ecstatic away support. Back on the ground he stood, arms outstretched, in front of the fans who chanted his name, tears in his eyes.

It was a heartfelt moment, not least because of the memories it brought back of his virtuoso performance in Amsterdam when he propelled his teammates to a Champions League final. For a moment, Spurs fans were transported away from a season of dismay to a time and place of unbridled happiness. That Lucas should hog the limelight, albeit briefly – rather than Kane – brought to mind one of the great 'what if' moments. What if he rather than a palpably unfit Kane had started the Champions League Final after scoring that stupendous semi-final hat-trick?

However, there is no doubt Kane was the heart and soul of the team. As Dan Kilpatrick wrote in the *London Evening Standard*, 'Kane's relentless quality and his importance to the club can scarcely be overstated; to score 30 (Premier League) goals (his equal best season) in this team is remarkable, and his goals have won 27 of Spurs' 60 points – or a staggering 45%.' He had scored against all Premier League opponents bar Bournemouth, West Ham and Manchester United, racked up more last-day goals than anyone in Premier League history and was the only player to reach the 30 mark twice since the Premier League comprised 20 clubs and 38 games in 1995/1996. (Surprisingly, on neither occasion did he secure the Golden Boot, finishing runner up to Mohamed Salah in 2017/2018 and Erling Haaland in 2022/2023.)

As the Spurs players acknowledged their supporters, the thought occurred to many of those watching that this could be a true hero bidding them farewell. Only Kane could put an end to the speculation. His exploits up front had been severely undermined by the fact that the team had conceded 63 goals, an average of more than 1.6 per match.

In the end, Spurs might have won handsomely, but Aston Villa had beaten Brighton and so took the

Europa Conference League spot. Spurs would be absent from any European competition for the first time since 2009/2010. When the board had responded dismissively to a request from the Tottenham Hotspur Supporters' Trust in January to outline its strategy, their reply had foolishly tempted fate: 'In the last 20 years the Club has qualified for European competition 17 times – 13 of which are currently successive – including six Champions League campaigns.' But that is now history. The harsh reality was that Tottenham Hotspur Football Club had completed a four-year journey from the sublime to the mediocre.

17. DREAM ON

After ENIC bought Tottenham Hotspur from Alan Sugar in January 2001 for £22 million, Daniel Levy made it his business to talk to a number of people associated with the club to help him get his feet under the table. So, when his executive assistant and wife, Tracy, called to arrange a meeting, Alex Fynn was happy to oblige and the two men met in ENIC's West End office later that month.

Fynn did most of the talking, chiefly regarding his work for the club in media and marketing for the Irving Scholar regime and for the FA in the creation of what became the Premier League. However, a couple of Levy comments struck home. George Graham should not be the Spurs manager, Levy said; he's an Arsenal man. And later on, with the objective of generating some initial positive PR, Levy suggested that what was needed was an ambassador to represent the club, someone like Gary Lineker.[44] Fynn reflected that whilst Levy might understand Arsenal's culture, he wasn't too clear about that of the club he now presided over.

Later that season, Fynn happened to meet Levy in the Arsenal boardroom on the occasion of the North

---

[44] Gary Lineker made almost twice as many appearances for Leicester City, the club he supports, as he did for Tottenham Hotspur.

London derby. Fynn told Levy how mistaken he was in thinking Gary Lineker might be a suitable representative for the club rather than a genuine Spurs hero like Pat Jennings, Martin Chivers or Gary Mabbutt. Unlike Lineker, all had current ties to the club as coaches or matchday hosts. Levy listened politely to the criticism and made no comment. And to this day, whilst still representing the club, these men of Tottenham are kept at arm's length from anything that may affect club policies.

On the credit side, though, Levy immediately showed some appreciation of his new club's heritage by emulating Irving Scholar and organising a second testimonial match for Bill Nicholson. (The first was in August 1983 against West Ham, and the second in 2001 against Fiorentina.) The poignant sight of an ailing Bill Nicholson supported by Martin Chivers should have given Levy cause to reflect on the close relationship between Tottenham's greatest manager and one of its all-time star players, and what roles such figures could play as prominent representatives and advisers.

In days gone by, both Arsenal and Spurs did things differently to most other clubs, adding a touch of class. In the Hill-Wood boardroom at Highbury, there were always flowers in the visiting team's colours (painted if necessary), while the Scholar regime – along with the Cobbolds at Ipswich[45] – was known for its hospitality. Douglas Alexiou, a director for 18 years and sometime chairman, was proudly claimed by Scholar as 'the best greeter in football'. Alexiou took his duties to heart, so much so that in heading up Spurs' delegations on their European excursions, he always made a point of thanking their hosts in their own languages. On one occasion, when Spurs played Hadjuk Split in the former Yugoslavia, Alexiou broke into song to perform a local folk tune, much to the astonishment and pleasure of his audience. Alexiou and fellow director Tony Berry continued the etiquette when Alan Sugar took over while they were on the board, although they ultimately lost their seats after promoting the return of Jürgen Klinsmann against Chairman Sugar's wishes in what turned out to be a successful bid to stave off regulation in 1997.[46]

For all the success that ENIC has achieved, there is a feeling that the character and traditions that once underpinned Tottenham Hotspur FC have been

---

[45] 'You ask what constitutes a crisis here? Well, if we ran out of white wine in the boardroom', said Ipswich chairman Patrick Cobbold in 1982.

[46] Jürgen Klinsmann scored nine goals in 15 loan appearances including a memorable quadruple in a crucial 6-2 victory over fellow relegation candidates Wimbledon.

allowed to fall by the wayside. Today, many feel the club has lost its way – the balance between business, sport and identity out of sync. During the Covid-19 pandemic, for example, the Government introduced a scheme whereby it paid 80% of an employee's salary up to £2,500 if the furloughed employees took a 20% wage cut. The club's decision to furlough 550 non-playing staff – no players were forced to take a pay cut – was greeted with uproar and public pressure forced its withdrawal. It left a lingering bad taste.

In recent years, the club has seen the departure of enough senior and long-serving staff for legitimate questions to be raised about why it has not been able, or willing, to retain their services. Head of Marketing Emma Taylor and Head of Retail Victoria Hawksley, both of whom had been at the club for 15 years and loved their jobs, have left, as well as the highly respected Head of Communications Simon Felstein. These departures followed perhaps more significant ones on the playing side. Academy Director John McDermott and Head of Football Operations Trevor Birch left in 2020, while Steve Hitchen, Director of Technical Performance, followed two years later. Alumni such as Darren Eales, Paul Barber and Paul Mitchell have gone on to bigger and better jobs at other clubs. So, when Scott Munn arrives as the Chief Football Officer in July 2023, he will have his work cut out on several fronts.

The level of discontent at the club must seem strange to outside observers. Unlike many Premier League clubs, Tottenham Hotspur is in rude financial health; the stadium is one of, if not the best in Europe, and the club consistently finishes in the top half of the world's richest football league. Today, 22 years into Daniel Levy's time as chairman, there can be no denying that he has been the driving force behind Tottenham Hotspur's evolution. However, his presence has become a hugely divisive issue. Perhaps what will always hang over the club is the paradox that whilst it was one of the prime movers in ushering in the money, money, money ethos that the modern game has embraced, it has been unable to capitalise fully on its pioneering work. A founder member of the Premier League 31 years ago, it has only once come close to winning it. And the club's financial strength has been overhauled by affluent, free-spending foreign owners.

A frequent criticism is that not enough money has been spent, but it is probably more accurate to say that it has too often been spent unwisely. Levy's attitude to transfers has been defined by his experience. As he told the students at Cambridge University, 'I know some fans and the media think we have to spend, spend, spend but every time Tottenham has done a big transfer, generally speaking, those players have not been the best-performing players. It's been the players we bought beneath the radar for not a lot of money who gave us the best performances.' This explains why successive managers were rarely able to acquire their first choices, who were invariably expensive.

Daniel Taylor detailed in *The Athletic* what happened after Dimitar Berbatov and Robbie Keane were sold. '(Juande) Ramos wanted to replace them with Samuel Eto'o from Barcelona and David Villa then at Valencia. Instead, Spurs signed Roman Pavlyuchenko from Spartak Moscow and Ramos was asked to put his trust in Darren Bent. who had joined the club the previous year from Charlton Athletic.' It ended in tears as Ramos himself told *The Athletic*, 'I proposed a series of players who we had to sign to reinforce the squad because they had sold Berbatov and Keane. They signed players who they thought were convenient. I didn't agree and those differences between one another led to my dismissal.' Ramos's experience was not atypical: Glenn Hoddle, Harry Redknapp and Mauricio Pochettino all failed to secure their first choices and were all fired when the fateful run of poor results occurred.

And while other clubs should never find it a pleasure to do business with Spurs, creating a situation where they are reluctant to do business at all is not helpful. The lingering resentment over what Manchester United considered was unnecessary brinkmanship involving the transfer of Berbatov being a case in point.

Too rarely are mistakes admitted by the current board, making it all the more difficult to learn from them. Under his predecessor, Alan Sugar, the counsel of senior players was sought, but Daniel Levy has rarely, if ever, done the same. Moreover, offers of help and suggestions from club heroes in times of crisis have fallen on deaf ears.

Perhaps most damning of all is the fact that the club failed to appreciate what it had when it finally – after years of frustration – got all its ducks in a row. Under Pochettino, it rediscovered its character and reconnected with fans in a way few had thought possible. It was traditional Tottenham for modern times. Or so it seemed. Pochettino's comment about the need for new furniture – which was never delivered – seems, with the benefit of hindsight, more accurate than ever and the consequences of failing to back the most successful manager since Keith Burkinshaw, over 30 years previously, have reverberated ever since. The quixotic decision to replace him with his coaching antithesis, José Mourinho, signalled the start of the unravelling of the progress that had taken Spurs to the position of perennial genuine title contenders and a Champions League final to a point where the most demoralising of seasons has just concluded in relegation form.

Spurs blogger Alan Fisher is invariably measured in his take on events, but he is particularly scathing about Levy, saying, 'It's tough being a leader, I understand that perfectly well, but hiding is not a good look. Such fireproof self-protection communicates weakness and indecision, as do his choices about managers. This runs right through the club, a lack of direction or plan. He has the vision and no idea how to achieve it, even after all these years. His capacity to not see what is happening around him smacks of remarkable self-delusion and lack of insight.'

Ironically, on the day former Prime Minister Boris Johnson stood down as a Member of Parliament, in his own mind blameless for the chaos he'd left behind, Levy was quoted as telling supporter groups, 'The notion that Tottenham haven't backed certain managers is incorrect. We're currently paying the price, perhaps, where some of the acquisitions have not turned out to be as we hoped.' What a contrast with Chelsea, where, to put it euphemistically, events had not worked out as the owners or supporters expected. The club issued a simple *mea culpa* in plain language. 'Clearly, for our men's team, it has been a disappointing season and there is a lot we can and will do better.'

So, for those supporters who have decided that leopards never change their spots, a new proprietor (and benefactor) is the only answer. The trouble is, it's not an option. There appears to be no one willing to meet the £5 billion ENIC is rumoured to value the club at. And even if there were suitors, the possibility that Daniel Levy might wish to retain an influential role could deter them. There are concerns, too, about what sort of owner would step forward in place of the current one. There is still some satisfaction to be derived from the fact that, for all the problems, Tottenham Hotspur is not possessed by a nation-state or dependent on the whim of a hedge fund focused on a profitable exit.

And already, some are wondering if they dare to dream again. Football marches on relentlessly through the calendar, and the new season fixtures list will be out with the old one barely packed away. There's a new head coach, too, Australian Ange Postecoglou, although doubts linger about whether he was the club's first choice.[47] Older heads will remember the headlines in the *London Evening Standard* that greeted another foreigner who arrived with Japanese experience to manage a North London club – 'Arsène who?'

After winning the Australian title as a player with his club South Melbourne, Postecoglou repeated the feat as a coach with both South Melbourne and Brisbane Roar and then, in charge of the national

---

[47] It took 72 days to make the appointment after Antonio Conte left in April, ironically the same time it took to appoint Nuno Espirito Santo who only survived for 10 Premier League matches. However, the new coach, unlike the unfortunate Nuno, will have a full preseason including a tour to his homeland Australia to settle in.

team, won the Asian Cup (the equivalent of the European Championships) and took them to qualification for the World Cup finals in 2018, before leaving to coach Yokohama F. Marinos in Japan. He made them J-League champions. Then, in Scotland, he helped Celtic secure five of the six domestic trophies available to them during his two-year tenure.

The situations Postecoglou inherited at Celtic and Spurs had much in common. An unfashionable choice by Celtic greeted with derision in some quarters – notably by the *Talksport* presenter, Alan Brazil (later forced to eat humble pie) – he took on a club that was floundering, overshadowed by its chief rival, with fan dissent directed at the boardroom, and which was desperately seeking to restore its identity through a traditional positive playing approach. He had succeeded in double-quick time in turning things around with Celtic, but now faced the same task with Tottenham on a much bigger stage at the age of 57, having never coached in one of Europe's top five leagues. However, unlike Mourinho and Conte, who gave the impression Spurs were lucky to have them, he saw the job as a step up and one he was desperately keen to make. Moreover, he appreciated the vital role of the fan base and that of a football club in its community.

Postecoglou is a leader and a realist. If Kane stays, there would be mutual pleasure in working together, but if he goes, the response will probably be that it doesn't concern him. What does matter is who he has to work with as of now. (As an early present to his new manager, Levy could tell Kane that he must see out his contract. And the conscientious Kane would, in all likelihood, play his heart out and maybe get Spurs into the Champions League – which would largely offset any fee to be derived from selling him now. And then he could re-sign or leave as a free agent.[48] Either way, he would always be a Tottenham hero.)

As for Levy himself, the word is that he might be 'stepping back'. It is unclear what this could involve, but it is unlikely that anyone else would be the final arbiter on important decisions while he remains at the club.

So, as the 2023/24 season beckons, are Tottenham Hotspur still dreaming? And what chance have dreams of becoming reality? There were real concerns as the previous campaign fell apart that a relegation battle could be the prospect for 2023/24. Those concerns will only grow if Kane is allowed to

---

[48] Under the new Champions League format from 2024-25, the number of participating clubs will increase from 32 to 36 which should ensure that there is an extra direct qualifier from the Premier League, five in total. The Premier League clubs should also benefit from the expected increase in the annual revenue of €1 billion from the current €3.6 billion.

leave and Postecoglou has his habitual slow start as the players get accustomed to his way of working. It is quite straightforward: if Plan A doesn't work, play it again, only better.[49]

On the other hand, Spurs remain better placed to succeed than most clubs. If those in charge, on and off the pitch, have a clear vision and stick to it, there is every reason to be optimistic. And despite the efforts of many proprietors to reduce the element of jeopardy so essential to making the Premier League the vibrant force it is, the view of the great Danny Blanchflower still resonates. Asked who he thought would win a game, he answered with words that fuel the dreams of all supporters at the start of a new season, 'I don't know, that's why they are playing the match.'

---

[49] The policy did not work in Europe where Celtic failed to progress beyond the group stages of the Europa League – subsequently being eliminated in the first knockout round of the Europa Conference League – and the Champions League. It won't be an issue he has to face in his first season in North London.

APPENDIX 1

Match Statistics 2022/2023

Game	Date	Opponents	Competition	Venue	Result	Score	League Position	Fraser FORSTER	Hugo LLORIS	Ben DAVIES	Clément LENGLET	Cristian ROMERO	Davinson SÁNCHEZ	Djed SPENCE	Emerson ROYAL	Eric DIER	
1	06/08/2022	Southampton	PL	H	W	4 - 1	1		nu		s	S		nu	nu	s	1
2	14/08/2022	Chelsea	PL	A	D	2 - 2	4		nu						nu	s	
3	20/08/2022	Wolves	PL	H	W	1 - 0	2		nu			nu					
4	28/08/2022	Nottm Forest	PL	A	W	2 - 0	3		nu			nu			S		
5	31/08/2022	West Ham	PL	A	D	1 - 1	3		nu			nu			nu		
6	03/09/2022	Fulham	PL	H	W	2 - 1	3		nu	nu					nu		
7	07/09/2022	Marseille	CLGS	H	W	2 - 0	2		nu		S	s	s	nu	nu	s	
8	13/09/2022	Sporting Lisbon	CLGS	A	L	0 - 2	2		nu			nu		nu	nu		
9	17/09/2022	Leicester	PL	H	W	6 - 2	2		nu				S	s		S	1
10	01/10/2022	Arsenal	PL	A	L	1 - 3	3		nu			s		S	nu	R	
11	04/10/2022	Eintracht Frankfurt	CLGS	A	D	0 - 0	3		nu		S	s		nu	nu		
12	08/10/2022	Brighton	PL	A	W	1 - 0	3		nu				nu	nu	nu		
13	12/10/2022	Eintracht Frankfurt	CLGS	H	W	3 - 2	3		nu		nu			S	nu		s
14	15/10/2022	Everton	PL	H	W	2 - 0	3		nu				nu	s	S	S	
15	19/10/2022	Man Utd	PL	A	L	0 - 2	3		nu				nu	S	S		s
16	23/10/2022	Newcastle	PL	H	L	1 - 2	3		nu		S	s		s	nu		
17	26/10/2022	Sporting Lisbon	CLGS	H	D	1 - 1	3		nu		s	S		nu	nu	S	
18	29/10/2022	Bournemouth	PL	A	W	3 - 2	3		nu			1		s	nu	s	S
19	01/11/2022	Marseille	CLGS	A	W	2 - 1	1		nu			1		nu	nu	S	
20	06/11/2022	Liverpool	PL	L	L	1 - 2	4		nu						nu	s	
21	09/11/2022	Nottm Forest	LC3	A	L	0 - 2		nu						S	nu		
22	12/11/2022	Leeds	PL	H	W	4 - 3	4		nu		1	s		S	nu	s	
23	26/12/2022	Brentford	PL	A	D	2 - 2	4		nu	S	s			S	nu		
24	01/01/2023	Aston Villa	PL	H	L	0 - 2	5		nu					nu	S	S	nu
25	04/01/2023	Crystal Palace	PL	A	W	4 - 0	5		nu		S	s		nu	nu	S	
26	07/01/2023	Portsmouth	FAC3	H	W	1 - 0		nu		nu	nu		S			
27	15/01/2023	Arsenal	PL	H	L	0 - 2	5		nu		S	s		nu	nu		
28	19/01/2023	Man City	PL	A	L	2 - 4	5		nu		s	S		nu	s1		
29	23/01/2023	Fulham	PL	A	W	1 - 0	5		nu			nu		nu			
30	28/01/2023	Preston	FAC4	A	W	3 - 0		nu						S	nu		
31	05/02/2023	Man City	PL	H	W	1 - 0	5		nu			nu		R	S		
32	11/02/2023	Leicester	PL	A	L	1 - 4	5		nu			nu			S	S	
33	14/02/2023	AC Milan	CLR16.1	A	L	0 - 1				S	s		nu			
34	19/02/2023	West Ham	PL	H	W	2 - 0	4				s			nu		1
35	26/02/2023	Chelsea	PL	H	W	2 - 0	4							nu		
36	01/03/2023	Sheff Utd	FAC5	A	L	0 - 1				nu	nu					
37	04/03/2023	Wolves	PL	A	L	0 - 1	4		s					nu	S	nu
38	08/03/2023	AC Milan	CLR16.2	H	D	0 - 0							R	S	s	
39	11/03/2023	Nottm Forest	PL	H	W	3 - 1	4							nu		
40	18/03/2023	Southampton	PL	A	D	3 - 3	4				s			nu	S	
41	03/04/2023	Everton	PL	A	D	1 - 1	4		nu			s			S	
42	08/04/2023	Brighton	PL	H	W	2 - 1	5		nu						nu	
43	15/04/2023	Bournemouth	PL	H	L	2 - 3	5		nu			s			Ss	
44	23/04/2023	Newcastle	PL	A	L	1 - 6	5	S	s	nu	nu		nu	nu		
45	27/04/2023	Man Utd	PL	H	D	2 - 2	5				S			nu		
46	30/04/2023	Liverpool	PL	A	L	3 - 4	6							nu	nu	
47	06/05/2023	Crystal Palace	PL	H	W	1 - 0	6				s			nu		S
48	13/05/2023	Aston Villa	PL	A	L	1 - 2	6				s			nu		
49	20/05/2023	Brentford	PL	H	L	1 - 3	8				s				s	nu
50	28/05/2023	Leeds	PL	A	W	4 - 1	8									

Matt DOHERTY	Bryan GIL	Dejan KULUSEVSKI	Lucas MOURA	Pierre-Emile HØJBJERG	Rodrigo BENTANCUR	Ryan SESSEGNON	Yves BISSOUMA	Harry KANE	Heung-Min SON	Ivan PERIŠIĆ	Japhet TANGANGA	RICHARLISON	Pape SARR	Oliver SKIPP	Harvey WHITE	Brandon AUSTIN	Alfie DEVINE	Romaine MUNDLE	Arnaut DANJUMA	Pedro PORRO	Alfie WHITEMAN	George ABBOTT	Matthew CRAIG	Yago SANTIAGO	Game
S	nu	s1	S		s	s1	S		S																1
nu	nu		S	1	s	s	S	1	s	S	nu	S													2
nu	nu	s	nu		S	S	1	s	s	nu	S														3
nu	s		s	S	S	2	s	s	nu	S	nu														4
nu	s			nu				nu	S	nu	nu														5
nu	S		1		nu	s1	s	S	nu		nu														6
S	nu	S		s	nu	S		s		S	2	nu	nu												7
nu	nu	S			nu	nu		s		nu		nu	nu												8
nu	nu	s		1		S	1	S3	s	nu	s		nu												9
S	nu		s		S	S	1p	s	s		s	nu	S												10
nu	S				S	nu			s	nu	nu	nu	nu												11
	nu				s	s1	s	S		S	nu	S													12
nu	S	S	s	s		S	1p	s2	nu		s	nu	S	nu											13
s	nu	S	1	s	nu	S	s1p				s		S												14
s	nu	S		s	S	s			s	nu		S													15
S	nu	S			s		1		S	nu		s	nu												16
s	S		s		1	nu	nu			nu		nu	nu	nu											17
nu	S		S		S1	s1	s		S	nu		s													18
nu	S		s	1	s	s	S		s	nu		nu	S	nu	nu										19
S	nu	S	S			s	s	1		nu		nu	S	nu											20
s	S	S		s	S		s		s	nu	S	nu	s												21
S	nu	s	S		2		S	1			nu	s		nu											22
	nu			1		nu		1			s		nu	nu	nu										23
s	s		s		S	s			s	nu		S	S												24
s1	s				S		2	1	s	nu		S	s	S											25
nu	s		nu		s	1						nu		S	nu										26
s	S	s			s	S			S	s	nu														27
nu	1			s	S	S			s	nu	S	nu													28
nu	s			nu	S	1	s		nu	S		nu													29
s	S		nu	s	s		nu	s2				S		nu		S1									30
	s			S	S	1	s	s		nu		nu		nu				nu	nu						31
	s	nu	s1			s	s	S	nu		nu		S	s											32
	s	nu				s		nu	S		nu	nu	S	nu	nu										33
	s	S			S1	S	nu	s	S	s		nu		nu	nu										34
	s	nu		1	S	nu	nu	s	nu	1	nu		nu	S											35
	S	s		S		nu	s	s	S	nu	nu		S	s											36
	s	S				nu	S	nu	nu		nu	s													37
	s	nu				nu	S	nu	nu	nu	nu		nu	S	nu										38
	S	S	2(1p)	s1	nu	nu	s	S	s		nu		nu	nu											39
	Ss	nu	1		S1	nu	s	S		nu		nu	s1												40
	SR		1p	s		nu		nu		nu	nu	nu	nu												41
	s		1	1	s	S	nu	S	s	nu	nu	nu	S												42
			1	nu	nu	s	nu	nu	S1					nu											43
	s		1	s	nu	S	s		nu	S															44
	S	nu	s1	s	S	s	nu		nu		nu	S	s1												45
	s	S	1	1	s	nu	S1	S	s	nu	nu	S	s												46
	S	nu		nu	1	s	nu	s	nu		nu		S												47
	S	nu		S	1p	S	s	nu	s	nu		S	s	nu											48
	s	S		1	S	nu	S	nu	nu		s	S		nu											49
	s	S1	s	2	s	nu	S	S	s	nu	nu	s1	S	S	nu										50

265

APPENDIX 2

Final Premier League Table 2022/2023

		Pld	W	D	L	GF	GA	GD	Pts
1	Manchester City	38	28	5	5	94	33	61	89
2	Arsenal	38	26	6	6	88	43	45	84
3	Manchester United	38	23	6	9	58	43	15	75
4	Newcastle United	38	19	14	5	68	33	35	71
5	Liverpool	38	19	10	9	75	47	28	67
6	Brighton & Hove Albion	38	18	8	12	72	53	19	62
7	Aston Villa	38	18	7	13	51	46	5	61
8	**Tottenham Hotspur**	**38**	**18**	**6**	**14**	**70**	**63**	**7**	**60**
9	Brentford	38	15	14	9	58	46	12	59
10	Fulham	38	15	7	16	55	53	2	52
11	Crystal Palace	38	11	12	15	40	49	-9	45
12	Chelsea	38	11	11	16	38	47	-9	44
13	Wolverhampton Wanderers	38	11	8	19	31	58	-27	41
14	West Ham United	38	11	7	20	42	55	-13	40
15	Bournemouth	38	11	6	21	37	71	-34	39
16	Nottingham Forest	38	9	11	18	38	68	-30	38
17	Everton	38	8	12	18	34	57	-23	36
18	Leicester City	38	9	7	22	51	68	-17	34
19	Leeds United	38	7	10	21	48	78	-30	31
20	Southampton	38	6	7	25	36	73	-37	25

APPENDIX 3

Transfers, Summer 2022, excluding loans and add-ons.

	Spent (£m)	Recouped (£m)	Net spend (£m)	No. of signings	No. of departures
Arsenal	113.5	20	93.5	5	9
Aston Villa	58.9	36.3	22.6	7	6
Bournemouth	22.7	0	22.7	6	1
Brentford	42.7	3	39.7	5	5
Brighton	32	97.5	-65.5	4	5
Chelsea	256.1	39.4	216.7	9	10
Crystal Palace	26.5	5	21.5	4	2
Everton	71.5	51	20.5	8	7
Fulham	54.2	19.7	34.5	11	8
Leeds	87.4	97	-9.6	8	6
Leicester	17	70.5	-53.5	2	2
Liverpool	73.2	60.3	12.9	4	7
Manchester City	119	150	-31	5	9
Manchester Utd	185.3	20.5	164.8	6	10
Newcastle	113	0	113	4	5
Nottingham Forest	133.35	5.05	128.3	23	14
Southampton	60.5	0	60.5	9	5
Tottenham	145.5	32.2	113.3	8	11
West Ham	158.6	15	143.6	8	5
Wolves	111	49.15	61.85	6	10
Total spend	1,881.95	183.45			

Summer Spending	Window (£m)	Deadline Day (£m)
2021	1,130.30	127.6
2020	1,220.50	120.9
2019	1,329.30	145.1
2018	1,235.15	115.1
2017	1,418.30	208.2
2016	1,177.90	152.95
2015	838.30	92.6
2014	853.50	84.5
2013	630	140
2012	490	110
2011	485	100
2010	365	35
2009	450	
2008	500	
2007	470	
2006	260	
2005	235	
2004	215	
2003	215	
2004	50	
2003	35	

Transfers, January 2023, excluding loans and add-ons.

	Spent (£m)	Recouped (£m)	Net spend (£m)	No. of signings	No. of departures
Arsenal	49.5	0	49.5	3	3
Aston Villa	28	12	16	2	4
Bournemouth	54.5	0	54.5	6	1
Brentford	0	0	0	1	1
Brighton	3.5	20	-16.5	1	2
Chelsea	284.5	12	272.5	8	2
Crystal Palace	9.7	0	9.7	2	1
Everton	0	46.5	-46.5	0	3
Fulham	8.8	0	8.8	2	2
Leeds	35.4	0	35.4	3	3
Leicester	28.2	0	28.2	3	2
Liverpool	37	0	37	1	0
Manchester City	8.2	0	8.2	1	2
Manchester Utd	0	0	0	3	2
Newcastle	48.3	0	48.3	3	3
Nottingham Forest	17.9	0	17.9	7	0
Southampton	61.55	0	61.55	5	0
Tottenham	0	0	0	2	3
West Ham	12	6.3	5.7	1	2
Wolves	32.4	0	32.4	5	2

Total spend	719.45	96.8

Previous Jan spending	Window (£m)	Deadline Day (£m)
2022	262.20	70.1
2021	65.50	6
2020	216.38	28.5
2019	114.40	37
2018	423.55	149.15
2017	208.04	63.6
2016	186.43	50
2015	127.13	45.33
2014	130	35
2013	120	35
2012	60	30
2011	225	135
2010	30	
2009	170	
2008	175	
2007	60	
2006	70	
2005	50	
2004	50	
2003	35	

Milton Keynes UK
Ingram Content Group UK Ltd.
UKHW012326100823
426697UK00006B/142